The Big Meal

Dan LeFranc

A Samuel French Acting Edition

SAMUELFRENCH.COM
SAMUELFRENCH-LONDON.CO.UK

Copyright © 2013 by Dan LeFranc

All Rights Reserved

Cover Design © by Bradford Louryk

THE BIG MEAL is fully protected under the copyright laws of the United States of America, the British Commonwealth, including Canada, and all other countries of the Copyright Union. All rights, including professional and amateur stage productions, recitation, lecturing, public reading, motion picture, radio broadcasting, television and the rights of translation into foreign languages are strictly reserved.

ISBN 978-0-573-70062-0

www.SamuelFrench.com
www.SamuelFrench-London.co.uk

FOR PRODUCTION ENQUIRIES

UNITED STATES AND CANADA
Info@SamuelFrench.com
1-866-598-8449

UNITED KINGDOM AND EUROPE
Theatre@SamuelFrench-London.co.uk
020-7255-4302

Each title is subject to availability from Samuel French, depending upon country of performance. Please be aware that may not be licensed by Samuel French in your territory. Professional and amateur producers should contact the nearest Samuel French office or licensing partner to verify availability.

CAUTION: Professional and amateur producers are hereby warned that *THE BIG MEAL* is subject to a licensing fee. Publication of this play(s) does not imply availability for performance. Both amateurs and professionals considering a production are strongly advised to apply to Samuel French before starting rehearsals, advertising, or booking a theatre. A licensing fee must be paid whether the title(s) is presented for charity or gain and whether or not admission is charged. Professional/Stock licensing fees are quoted upon application to Samuel French.

No one shall make any changes in this title(s) for the purpose of production. No part of this book may be reproduced, stored in a retrieval system, or transmitted in any form, by any means, now known or yet to be invented, including mechanical, electronic, photocopying, recording, videotaping, or otherwise, without the prior written permission of the publisher. No one shall upload this title(s), or part of this title(s), to any social media websites.

For all enquiries regarding motion picture, television, and other media rights, please contact Samuel French.

MUSIC USE NOTE

Licensees are solely responsible for obtaining formal written permission from copyright owners to use copyrighted music in the performance of this play and are strongly cautioned to do so. If no such permission is obtained by the licensee, then the licensee must use only original music that the licensee owns and controls. Licensees are solely responsible and liable for all music clearances and shall indemnify the copyright owners of the play(s) and their licensing agent, Samuel French, against any costs, expenses, losses and liabilities arising from the use of music by licensees. Please contact the appropriate music licensing authority in your territory for the rights to any incidental music.

IMPORTANT BILLING AND CREDIT REQUIREMENTS

If you have obtained performance rights to this title, please refer to your licensing agreement for important billing and credit requirements.

THE BIG MEAL had its New York premeire produced by Playwrights Horizons at the Peter Jay Sharp Theater on March 21, 2012. The performance was directed by Sam Gold, with scenic and costume design by David Zinn and lights by Mark Barton. The Production Stage Manager was Alaina Taylor. The cast was as follows:

WOMAN #1 .... ANITA GILLETTE
MAN #1 .... TOM BLOOM
WOMAN #2 .... JENNIFER MUDGE
MAN #2 .... DAVID WILSON BARNES
WOMAN #3 .... PHOEBE STROLE
MAN #3 .... CAMERON SCOGGINS
GIRL .... RACHEL RESHEFF
BOY .... GRIFFIN BIRNEY
SERVER .... MOLLY WARD

THE BIG MEAL was produced by the Studio Theatre in Washington, D.C on May 1, 2012. The performance was directed by Johanna Gruenhut, with assistance from Brian Crane, sets by Tim Mackabee, costumes by Addy Diaz, sound by Elisheba Ittoop, and lights by John Burkland. The cast was as follows:

WOMAN #1 .... ANNIE HOUSTON
MAN #1 .... MATT DOUGHERTY
WOMAN #2 .... HYLA MATTHEWS
MAN #2 .... CHRIS GENEBACH
WOMAN #3 .... ASHLEY DILLARD
MAN #3 .... JOSH ADAMS
GIRL .... MAYA BRETTELL
BOY .... SAM O' BRIEN

THE BIG MEAL had its world premiere produced by the American Theatre company in Chicago on March 3, 2011. The performance was directed by Dexter Bullard, and the Associate Director was Jason W. Gerace. Scenic and lighting design was by Brian Sidney Bembridge. Costume design was Tif Bullard, with sound design by Kevin O'donnel. The Production Stage Manager was Dana M. Nestrick. The cast was as follows:

WOMAN #1 .... Peggy Roeder
MAN #1 .... Will Zahrn
WOMAN #2 .... Lia D. Mortensen
MAN #2 .... Philip Earl Johnson
WOMAN #3 .... Lindsay Leopold
MAN #3 .... Andrew Goetten
GIRL .... Emily Leahy
BOY .... Noah Jerome Schwartz

CAST OF CHARACTERS

WOMAN #1 (Older Woman)
    NICOLE (Older Woman)
    ALICE, Sam's mother

WOMAN #2 (Woman)
    NICOLE (Woman)
    MADDIE, Sam & Nicole's daughter (Woman)
    JACKIE, Robbie & Stephanie's daughter (Woman)

WOMAN #3 (Young Woman)
    NICOLE (Young Woman)
    JESSICA, a gentle soul
    MADDIE, Sam & Nicole's daughter (Young Woman)
    STEPHANIE, Robbie's wife (Young Woman)
    JACKIE, Robbie & Stephanie's daughter (Young Woman)

GIRL
    PESKY LITTLE GIRL
    MADDIE, Sam & Nicole's daughter (Girl)
    JACKIE, Robbie & Stephanie's daughter (Girl)

MAN #1 (Older Man)
    SAM (Older Man)
    ROBERT, Sam's father
    JACK, Stephanie's father

MAN #2 (Man)
    SAM (Man)
    ROBBIE, Sam & Nicole's son (Man)

MAN #3 (Young Man)
    SAM (Young Man)
    ROBBIE, Sam & Nicole's son (Young Man)
    MADDIE'S ADOLESCENT BOYFRIENDS,
        Steven, Marcus, Jeremy, Patrick, Michael
    SAMMY, Maddie's son (Young Man)

BOY
    PESKY LITTLE BOY
    ROBBIE, Sam & Nicole's son (Boy)
    SAMMY, Maddie's son (Boy)
    MATTHEW, Jackie's son

PLAYWRIGHT'S NOTES

The setting is a restaurant in the Midwestern United States, or rather, every restaurant in the Midwestern United States. Some are popular chains, others are more homely; very few are fancy.

There are tables ready to be sat. They may be brought together or apart depending on the size of the party at any given moment.

Eight actors total. Three men. Three women. A boy and a girl. The server is probably a stagehand.

The actors play the multiple generations of one family as they glide through time (and the guests they pick up along the way). As the characters age, their "essences" pass from younger to older actors. These "passes" ought to be performed as simply as possible. They are designated in the script by the character's name sliding into a new column.

Shifts in time are designated by (SHIFT). These can be indicated as subtly or conspicuously as the moment demands, but please try not to overdo the theatrics. These are placed in the script primarily to help the actors, not the audience. We don't want the audience to get lost, of course, but it's okay if they're occasionally a little behind the play.

The food probably doesn't look very appetizing. Colorful. Glistening. Grotesque.

Except for a few key moments (and one long stretch towards the end), the play moves very quickly. Pretend the cast is an orchestra tasked to play a piece of music for a conductor whose pace is brisk and unrelenting. Or pretend they're sitting together at a player piano. Or getting their cues from a rapidly-scrolling teleprompter. Regardless of which metaphor serves you best, play the action on the line. At performance speed, the play ought to run roughly eighty minutes.

Do your best to cast an ensemble who feels like a family, but don't break your back to make everyone look related.

Let the language carry us through time and space. Don't worry about representing the various restaurants literally. The scenography should probably be a little abstract, allowing our imaginations to leave the confines of a restaurant from time to time. Big scenic gestures should be kept to a minimum (or preferably, completely avoided). As a rule, there should be as few objects flying around the set as possible. The only plates in the play should be the ones that land in the script. The only consumables should be the ones on those plates. Feel free to rearrange the furniture when necessary, but let our imaginations do the heavy lifting.

Don't worry about having the server bring out the drinks. Use minimal glassware and let the audience imagine whatever it is the characters might be drinking at any given moment. This is another way of saying you don't need to fill them up. It's probably best to use "neutral" glasses, with maybe a wine or margarita glass thrown in as the play progresses. The same small collection of glasses can be used throughout the entire play, and actors can hang onto them throughout the various (SHIFTS). A shift in time does not necessarily mean a shift in glassware.

Lines in ( ) are meant to be spoken to another character more privately than publicly.

A large generational gap between the actors is important to understanding the story. In other words, if possible cast children in the youngest roles; not teenagers.

The duration of the meals can vary depending on the needs of the production. The first and last meals should probably be the longest. The dialogue might begin over some of the later meals in order to break up the rhythm of the device. But see what works best given the circumstances.

There's a lot of cross-talk in this play and some parts of the conversations are more important than others. Make sure to highlight the parts that are most crucial to the story. It might be helpful to identify the "A conversations" and "B conversations" throughout.

Sound and light cues should be kept to an absolute minimum. There's a moment of dancing that might require a song but that's about it for sound. Lighting may be used more often but see how little you can get away with and take it from there.

This is key: all of the actors should be on stage for the entire play. When not in a scene, they are probably sitting in an area where they are removed from the action but can also observe it—actively waiting for their moment to jump in.

WOMAN #1	MAN #1	WOMAN #2	MAN #2	WOMAN #3	MAN #3	GIRL	BOY
				(she is setting a table. not interested in him.) **NICOLE.** *(she cleans his table, ignoring him.)*	*(he is sitting at a table by himself with a drink.)* **SAM.** … … am I in your way?		
				pretty much	*(he drinks)* so what's up?		
				um side work			
				yeah cuz I work here	side work huh? okay		
				and I don't want to waste any more of my life than I have to			
				what?	*(he drinks.)* then don't		
				is it?	uh if you don't want to waster your life then…don't it's pretty simple		
				doable *(smiles)*	yeah I mean no it's really hard but it's uh…doable I think yeah		

1

WOMAN #1	MAN #1	WOMAN #2	MAN #2	WOMAN #3	MAN #3	GIRL	BOY
					(…*smiles back uncertainly*)		
					is there like		
					something on my face?		
				(SHIFT)	**(SHIFT)**		
				hey			
					hi		
				sorry I'm late			
					it's okay		
					you wanna sit down?		
				oh yeah thanks			
					here let me get your		
					chair		
				oh you don't have to	(*he does*)		
				okay			
				wow			
				chivalry			
				that's intense			
					okay–		
				what's your name			
				again?			
					my?		
					Sam		
					my name's Sam		
				I thought it was			
				something else			
					I'm pretty sure it's Sam		
				I'm Nicky			
					oh yeah I know		
				my parents named me			
				Nicole but just look at			
				what your mouth does			
				when you say it			
				Nicole			
				it's weird			
					I think it's pretty		
				yeah			
				you would			
				you totally would			
					okay		
				well not uh			
				alright			
				so not to be upfront			

WOMAN #1	MAN #1	WOMAN #2	MAN #2	WOMAN #3	MAN #3	GIRL	BOY
				but I uh I'm not really looking for anything serious right now			
					oh yeah did it seem like I–?		
				no no no no I just wanna be clear cuz I just got out of this long term thing with this total um clingy narcissistic asshole and I'm looking for you know someone to pass the time with or whatever but not like a "relationship"	no I get it it's cool		
					oh yeah "relationships" they're so		
				you know what I mean?			
					yeah it's like I look at my parents and they're I don't know intense I guess and uh hopefully you'll never meet them so		
				yeah I don't anticipate meeting your parents			
					yeah		
				this is totally casual			
					yeah		
				so that means if this goes anywhere beyond tonight which I'm not saying it will we should keep this as			

THE BIG MEAL

WOMAN #1	MAN #1	WOMAN #2	MAN #2	WOMAN #3	MAN #3	GIRL	BOY
				uh			
				as anonymous as			
				possible			
				you know?			
				like	sure		
				I don't really wanna			
				know about your life			
				and I really REALLY	oh okay		
				don't want you to			
				know about mine			
					cool		
					that's cool		
				(pause)	*(pause)*		
					but I can ask you what		
					you like to drink?		
				oh oh yeah sorry yeah	cuz I really wanna buy		
					you a drink *(smiles)*		
				(smiles)			
				yeah okay let's have a			
				drink			
					cool		
				(drinks)	*(drinks)*		
					how is it?		
				good			
					yeah I really like this		
					one		
				(pause)	*(pause)*		
				you wanna get out of	should we order–?		
				here?			
					what?		
				you wanna mess			
				around?			
					uh…I am a male		
				like right now?			
				cuz no offense but this	uh		
				date is kinda painful			
					yeah yeah		
				then let's go			
				(SHIFT)	**(SHIFT)**		
					hey Nicky		

WOMAN #1	MAN #1	WOMAN #2	MAN #2	WOMAN #3	MAN #3	GIRL	BOY
				Sam			
					sorry I'm		
				it's okay			
					I'm glad you called		
				yeah well I was pretty bored so…			
					did you order?		
				just a drink you want one?			
					sure		
				(drinks)	*(drinks)* this is good		
				it's kinda weak			
					yeah you know my mom claims to have invented the Cadillac Margarita		
				oh yeah?			
					yeah		
				is that a margarita you order at a drive-in or–?			
					no haha that's funny but uh no it's just like a normal margarita but with uh a splash of Gran Marnier		
				cool cool			
					yeah she's really proud of it for some reason		
				so is your mom like an alcoholic inventor?			
					(smiles) uh well maybe like casually alcoholic but no she's just she works in restaurants		

WOMAN #1	MAN #1	WOMAN #2	MAN #2	WOMAN #3	MAN #3	GIRL	BOY
				yeah so's my sister			
					you have a sister?		
				yeah			
				actually the place where			
				I work			
				where you um			
				picked me up			
				she's the manager and	is that what you'd call		
				pretty much the	it?		
				only reason I	a pick up?		
					like I just dragged you		
				haha yeah kinda	out of the bar by your		
				yeah	hair back to your		
					apartment?		
				well except I was the			
				one doing the dragging			
					(smiles) yeah yeah		
					hey do you think your		
					roommate woke up?		
				I hope so I hate that			
				bitch			
					(laughs) why?		
				she's very you know			
				(gesture)			
				very *(gesture)*			
				like this one time my			
				sister came over to			
				cook and she was uh			
				wow okay			
					what?		
				I am telling you stuff			
				about my life			
				I don't know why I am	oh		
				telling you stuff about			
				my life	it's okay		
				cuz this thing			
				this thing is not–			
					totally		
				(SHIFT)	**(SHIFT)**		
					Nicky		
				hey Sam			
				(they kiss passionately)			
					how's your sister?		

WOMAN #1	MAN #1	WOMAN #2	MAN #2	WOMAN #3	MAN #3	GIRL	BOY
				she's good			
				she left this morning			
					that was fun hanging out		
					she's cool		
				yeah she liked you too			
					you want a–*(drink gesture)*?		
				what do you think?			
					haha		
				(drinks)	*(drinks)*		
				this is good			
					I know		
				your mom's a genius			
					you think so?		
				this drink's awesome			
					yeah she can definitely make a drink		
				you're kind of awesome too			
					what?		
				(she makes a face)			
					(laughs)		
				(SHIFT)	**(SHIFT)**	**(SHIFT)**	
						(the sound of a child crying in the restaurant)	
						eeeeee	
					whoa	eeee	
						ee	
						eeeeee	
						eeee	
						ee	
						eeeeeee	
					sounds like some kind of freakish animal	eeee	
				is that a kid?			
				have you ever heard a gibbon?			
						ee	
					what's a gibbon?	eeeee	
						e	
				you've never been to the zoo?			

WOMAN #1	MAN #1	WOMAN #2	MAN #2	WOMAN #3	MAN #3	GIRL	BOY
					yeah but	eeee	
						ee	
				well they're like monkeys but they're apes		e	
						ee	
						e	
					what's the difference?	e	
				apes don't have tails			
						ee	
					really?		
						e	
				listen to that			
						eee	
					wow		
						ee	
				do you like kids?		e	
						e	
					they're okay	ee	
						eee	
				I hate kids they're nothing but like snot and shit		e	
						eeeeeeeee	
				seriously	(laughs)		
				I think thier bodies are literally powered by mucus		eeee	
						eeeee	
					(as if by accident) I love you	ee	
				what?		eeeee	
						e	
					what?	eee	
						eeee	
				(SHIFT)	**(SHIFT)**	**(SHIFT)**	
				yeah so I don't know what to do			
					she still won't move out?		
				no she's a freak *(drinks)*	did you call the landlord?		
				yeah I called the landlord			

WOMAN #1	MAN #1	WOMAN #2	MAN #2	WOMAN #3	MAN #3	GIRL	BOY
				but the thing is she's on the lease and she hasn't technically done anything so there's not much I can–	okay do you think you can wait it out?		
				wait it? no Sam this is ruining my life it is ruining my life I hate her I	okay okay so do you want me to talk to her?		
				really? you'd talk to her?	yeah I mean it's worth a shot right?		
				okay …but I think she's kind of obsessed with you so don't let her touch your hair or anything	she's? whoa seriously?		
				yeah a little …I mean can you blame her?			
				(makes a face) **(SHIFT)**	*(smiles)* **(SHIFT)**		
					so what do you think? nice right?		
				are you sure we can afford this? it's pretty fancy	yeah I got it I mean my credit card's got it		
				no you can't pay for this the glasses are like			

WOMAN #1	MAN #1	WOMAN #2	MAN #2	WOMAN #3	MAN #3	GIRL	BOY
				actual glass	but whatever it's our anniversary		
				(jokingly) anniversary? is that what this is?			
					uh huh		
				of what? the first time we like coupled?			
					um no of our uh *(conspiratorial playfulness)* relationship		
				(conspires back) relationship? we're in a relationship?			
					(keeps it up) yeah		
				(so does she) holy shit			
					I know		
				how the hell did that happen?			
					that's classified information		
				I have clearance			
					lemme see it		
				(she lowers a shoulder strap)			
					good enough		
				now tell me			
					well first we met		
				then what?			
					then we liked each other		
				interesting			
					then we…coupled		
				I liked that part			
					me too		
				and then?			
					we fell in love		
				oh yeah			

WOMAN #1	MAN #1	WOMAN #2	MAN #2	WOMAN #3	MAN #3	GIRL	BOY
				that was awesome what happens next?			
					I can tell you but I'm gonna need to see some more clear- ance		
				(SHIFT)	**(SHIFT)**		
				you want a drink?			
					that's cool		
				…	…		
				so what's up?			
					nothing		
				nothing's up? we haven't talked in a week			
					yeah?		
				so is there something we need to talk about? now?			
					like what?		
				like I don't know anything everything			
					uh…		
				(pause) what the fuck Sam?	*(pause)*		
					what?		
				say it			
					say what?		
				(she starts to cry) oh my god say it say it just say it!			
				(SHIFT)	**(SHIFT)**		

WOMAN #1	MAN #1	WOMAN #2	MAN #2	WOMAN #3	MAN #3	GIRL	BOY
					you want another *(gestures)*?		
				(shrugs)			
					so then do you wanna get outta here or–?		
				look I can't keep doing this			
					okay		
				we're not involved but then I see you and then we are and it gets confusing			
					yeah well my dad says this thing about healing		
				I don't wanna hear about your dad	how it's like		
					he's a smart guy		
				you don't even like him			
					yeah I do		
				since when?			
					he's my dad		
				you don't have to like your dad			
					I didn't say I had to		
				right			
					you're drunk		
				well you're a waste of my fucking time			
					okay then …forget it		
				forget it?			
					yeah		
				… is that what you want?	…		
					sounds like it's what you want		
				… …asshole			

WOMAN #1	MAN #1	WOMAN #2 (SHIFT)	MAN #2 (SHIFT)	WOMAN #3 (SHIFT)	MAN #3 (SHIFT)	GIRL	BOY
		NICOLE hey Sam	**SAM** Nicky wow what are you doing here?				
		can I sit down? sorry if I'm	uh sure no it's okay you uh …you look great				
		thanks you look pretty much exactly like yourself which is a good thing it's totally a good thing	 oh really? cuz I mean it's been a while				
		a little while yeah	how are you?				
		good I'm good I'm uh here with this guy	 oh yeah me too I mean I'm not here with a guy I'm uh				
		she cool?	yeah she's great she's very um peeing she's peeing what about your uh				
		he's very um peeing too	 good				

WOMAN #1	MAN #1	WOMAN #2	MAN #2	WOMAN #3	MAN #3	GIRL	BOY
			that's uh great				
			I'm really happy for you				
			(smiles)				
		(smiles)					
		(pause)	*(pause)*				
		you wanna get out of here?	well it was great to–				
			what?				
		this guy sucks					
			whoa				
			Nicky				
			hey				
			look				
			this woman				
			she's–				
		oh					
			no Nicky				
			she's				
		it's okay					
		I get it					
			she sucks okay?				
			she sucks				
			but she's nice so I feel				
			like I should prob-				
			ably…				
			not be an asshole				
		chivalry	which I believe is the				
			last thing you called me				
		yeah something like that					
			…but um				
			maybe				
			later tonight				
			you and I can uh				
		(SHIFT)	**(SHIFT)**				
		hey					
			did you order?				
		no I just got here					
			you look um				
			awesome as always				

WOMAN #1	MAN #1	WOMAN #2	MAN #2	WOMAN #3	MAN #3	GIRL	BOY
		thanks					
			so I didn't really have time to ask the other night–				
		no there wasn't much time to do anything but uh *(smiles)*					
			(smiles) yeah				
		you got better					
			really?				
		uh huh					
			well I have been prac-ticing				
		oh really?					
			sure but not like a lot I mean I did keep busy but uh forget it reset ha ha …um				
		so					
			how's your sister?				
		she's good					
			is she still working in um restaurants or?				
		basically she's more like behind the scenes now …purchasing					
			cool cool …is she like…married?				
		uh no no way I mean why would anyone do that to themselves? like marriage is so *(gestures)*					
			oh				
			yeah yeah				
		you know?					

WOMAN #1	MAN #1	WOMAN #2	MAN #2	WOMAN #3	MAN #3	GIRL	BOY
			I…fully agree				
		(SHIFT)	**(SHIFT)**				
		Sam					
			hey				
		sorry I'm					
			it's okay				
		(they kiss across the table)					
			oh hold on Nic				
		what?	you've got something in your hair				
		I do?					
			yeah				
			huh				
			what is?				
			gee where did this come from?				
			(he removes a small shiny ring)				
		what uh?					
		what is that?					
		Sam?					
		what the hell is that?					
			so I know it might seem a little um fast				
		what are you doing?	I mean kinda fast but not really fast cuz well we have known each other for quite a while				
		Sam	and I know we both have like issues with the institution or whatever				
		are you really fucking doing this?	but I figure some things are worth the risk				
		oh my god Sam seriously?					
			yeah				
		I'm not wearing underwear					
			you're not?				

WOMAN #1	MAN #1	WOMAN #2	MAN #2	WOMAN #3	MAN #3	GIRL	BOY
		no this dress isn't– don't you think I should be wearing underwear for this?					
			uh should we order you some? haha				
		don't don't say things like that					
			right				
		would we have to have a "wedding"? cuz I really…I really hate weddings they're so *(makes a face)* you know?	uh well				
			does that mean you're gonna say yes?				
		I don't know now there are people watching I used to work here this isn't exactly anonymous like that waiter over there? I think I maybe made out with that waiter once oh god I can't believe he still works here	I know that's why I'm doing this here it's where we met really? *(he laughs)*				
		yeah	Nicky				
		at least don't do the knee thing	what are you talking about? I have to do the knee thing				

WOMAN #1	MAN #1	WOMAN #2	MAN #2	WOMAN #3	MAN #3	GIRL	BOY
		yeah but then you're gonna be kinda looking up my dress and that doesn't seem like the most uh–					
		plus I always thought you might if you did this which I never expected you to cuz that's *(crazy gesture)* and I'm not *(crazy gesture)* if you did pop the the thing in my mind I thought you'd maybe	yeah okay				
		just take my hand and… pop the thing but not the thing thing you'd say something like the thing but better than the thing way more interesting than the thing cuz it shouldn't be like a movie thing it should be like	what?				
		like something real um beautiful? different I don't know	like what?				
			so um how about this? *(he takes her hand. maybe cautiously slips the ring onto her finger.)*				

WOMAN #1	MAN #1	WOMAN #2	MAN #2	WOMAN #3	MAN #3	GIRL	BOY
			how's that?				
		oh Jesus christ					
		yes!					
		yes!					
		FUCKING YES!					
		(they kiss across the table like maniacs)					
		(SHIFT)	**(SHIFT)**				
		(they curl into each other. sigh.)					
			you think we're being like obnoxious?				
		a little					
			like maybe we shouldn't be making out in public like this?				
		probably not					
			(smiles) if I were in this place I'd hate us but we're us so I'm into it				
		definitely *(bites his ear)*					
			so what do you wanna do now?				
		mmm everything					
			everything?				
		yeah ...well except for kids					
			right				
		cuz who would do that to themselves?					
			crazy people our parents				
		I mean just think about it					

WOMAN #1	MAN #1	WOMAN #2	MAN #2	WOMAN #3	MAN #3	GIRL	BOY
		a whole life with just each other think about how fucking rad that sounds					
			sounds pretty fucking rad				
		yeah we could like go places together					
			you mean like Dayton or–?				
		no dumbass					
			hey				
		(she takes his hand) like places that are really places like like Barcelona *(she pronounces it in a fakey-funny-Castillian accent)*					
			Barcelona *(so does he. they keep this up)* wow that is…exotic				
		it is					
			what does one do in Barcelona?				
		in Barcelona one can do everything					
			everything? that sounds like a lot				
		yes but in Barcelona it is not so much					
			(laughs)				
						LITTLE GIRL *(far away)* eeeeeee eeeee	**LITTLE BOY** *(far away)* eeeeeee eeee
			what was that?				eeeeeee eeee
		must be someone's kids					
			it sounds like some			eeeeeee	

THE BIG MEAL

WOMAN #1	MAN #1	WOMAN #2	MAN #2	WOMAN #3	MAN #3	GIRL	BOY
			kind of animal			eeee	e
						eeeeeeee	eeeee
						~~eeeee~~	ee
							eee
		I think they're kinda cute				eeee	e
						e	ee
			you hate kids			ee	
							eeeeeee
							eee
		me? you're the one who hates kids				eeeee	eeeeeeee
			when did I say that?				
		you know *(gestures)*					eeeeeee
							eee
							eeeeeeee
						(closer) eeeeeee	
						eeeee	
						eeeeeee	
						eeeee	
						eeeeeee	*(closer)* eeeeeeeee
						eeeee	eee
						eeeeeeee	eeeeeeeee
			okay my body is literally shaking			eeeeee	
						eeeeeeeee	
						eee	
						eeeeeeeeeee	
						eeeeeeee	eeeeeee
		yeah				eeeee	eee
						eee	eeeeeeeeeee
			you wanna get out of here?			eeeeeeee	eeeeeeee
						eeeeeeeeeeeee	eeeeeeeee
						EEEEEEE EEEEEE!	EEEEEEEEE EEEEEE!
		(SHIFT)	**(SHIFT)**			**(SHIFT)**	**(SHIFT)**
						(GIRL runs on. she leaps into NICOLE's lap.)	*(BOY runs on. he leaps into SAM's lap.)*
		oh my god who is this? whose child is this? hello?	whoa				
		did someone lose a child?	hello? did someone lose a child?				

Loud! (handwritten annotation)

WOMAN #1	MAN #1	WOMAN #2	MAN #2	WOMAN #3	MAN #3	GIRL	BOY
			I've got a parentless child here!				
			hello?				
			anyone?				
		hello?					
		anyone?					
			anyone?				
						MADDIE.	
						mom	
		has someone lost a little booger monster?					
		I've got a booger monster here	I've got a Tazmanian devil who likes to get tickled				
							ROBBIE.
							(laughs)
							dad
							dad
							no
		look at all those boogers				*(laughs)* I don't have boogers	no
							dad
		(she tickles GIRL some more.)	*(he tickles BOY some more)*			*(laughs)*	*(laughs)*
			you guys hungry?				
						yeah	
							yessss
			yesssss?				
			yessss?				
			what are you a python?				
							yessss
						I'm a tamarin	
		tamarin					
		very good Maddie					
		and what's a tamarin got that a gibbon doesn't?					yesssss
			what's a python sound like?				
						a tail	
							yeeesssss
		alright kiddo					
		you've won the grand prize					
						is the grand prize crayons?	

WOMAN #1	MAN #1	WOMAN #2	MAN #2	WOMAN #3	MAN #3	GIRL	BOY
							yeeesssss
		you don't like crayons?	okay that's enough python, buddy				
						that's what the grand prize was last time	yeeesssss
		well there's a limited selection of grand prizes these days					
			come here sit here next to your dad				
						why?	
		well because of Congress					
						why? what'd the contest do?	
							can I get a corndog?
		the contest passed a bill					
						what's a bill?	
			no				
		a bill's like a band-aid					
							why not?
						okay	
			cuz you had a corndog last night				
		he wants a corndog? no corndogs					so?
		you know what they're made out of?					why?
		no they're made out of pigs and not the nice parts of pigs					hot dogs
							but I don't like anything else
						Jennifer's mom has a pet pig	
		you like tostadas					
						dad	they're alright
						Jennifer's mom has a pet pig	
			I heard you, honey				

WOMAN #1	MAN #1	WOMAN #2	MAN #2	WOMAN #3	MAN #3	GIRL	BOY
			what do you want to eat?			Jennifer says her mom likes to go outside and smoke and talk to her pet pig	I'd rather have a corndog
		sorry kiddo you're getting something else					
							there's nothing else to get
		I'm sure you'll find something					
			well that's what happens when you do what Jennifer's mom did when she was young you end up talking to your pet pig				
						I want a pet pig can I have a pet pig?	
			we don't have room for a pet pig now come on honey what do you want?				
		hey Sam					if we had a pig I bet we'd have bacon all the time
			yeah?				
		can I ask you something?					
			yup				
						pigs make bacon?	
							yeah they poo it out
		you think you can maybe take off work on Wednesday?					
						no they don't	
							uh huh bacon poo
			Wednesday? uh maybe …hold on Maddie			dad …daddy do pigs poo bacon?	
							say yes
			(smiles) hey mom? do pigs poo bacon?				
		(smiles. laughs a little.) Robbie					

WOMAN #1	MAN #1	WOMAN #2	MAN #2	WOMAN #3	MAN #3	GIRL	BOY
		that is very funny but very gross stop taunting your sister and figure out your order					
			what's on Wednesday?				you're no fun
		it's just this wine tasting thing a promo for this new restaurant some of my girlfriends were talking about	okay			told you	
							she didn't say no
							it's still possible
		it sounds fun					
			you can't do it Thursday?				
		I work on Thursday					
			yeah I know and I work Wednesday			(she colors. makes sounds)	
			why can't you take off Thursday?				
		because a temp's coming in Thursday amd I need to make sure he doesn't blow up the office				wah	
						wah	
			so you want me to ditch work so you can get buzzed with your friends in the middle of the afternoon?			wah	
		it's a wine tasting …Maddie honey enough with the (gestures)				wah	
						sorry	
		it's fine just don't do it anymore okay? not all sounds are fun sounds					
			can't your sister watch the kids?				

WOMAN #1	MAN #1	WOMAN #2	MAN #2	WOMAN #3	MAN #3	GIRL	BOY
		how many times are we gonna make her do that, Sam? seriously she's my sister not our babysitter	make her?				
			she loves the kids and who wouldn't? who wouldn't love you little rascals? huh?				
							(makes a pig sound)
			(makes a pig sound back at him)				
		well I think she's beginning to feel a little put out					*(pig sound)*
			okay okay I'll take off Wednesday				*(pig sound)*
		great I appreciate it				*(pig sound!)*	
							that's wrong
			you know why? because you deserve it you really do				
		thank you					we weren't doing pigs
			I'm sorry for arguing			you were so doing pigs! dad! dad! dad! daddy! dad! weren't you doing pigs?	
		just don't make me nag I hate feeling like a nag					
			yeah honey we were doing pigs				
						see?	
			I love you				I'm reading my menu
		I love you too				fine *(she reads hers too)*	*(he does)*
		(they kiss the air but not each other) mwah! **(SHIFT)**	mwah! **(SHIFT)** you guys hungry?			**(SHIFT)** *(monkey sounds)*	**(SHIFT)**

WOMAN #1	MAN #1	WOMAN #2	MAN #2	WOMAN #3	MAN #3	GIRL	BOY
		what are you a tamarin?					
							mom
		what is it Robbie?					
							what's an enchilada?
		hey you know what an enchilada is? it's a Mexican corndog					
							it is?
		yep! *(they secretly high five each other)*					
							but I thought Mexicans only ate real dogs
		Robbie!					
							what? they do! Mexicans eat dogs! it's a fact!
		well that's a bunch of crap					
			Nicky–				
		what? no listen to this	hey watch your mouth around him okay?				
		where'd you hear that?					
		Robbie					
							it's top secret
		you wanna be grounded?					
							it is! I swore!
		of course of course you did son of a bitch					
			Nicky				
							…grandpa
		what?				grandpa told me something too you wanna hear?	
			not now honey				
		he's polluting thier minds, Sam your father is polluting their minds with this this (bullshit)					

WOMAN #1	MAN #1	WOMAN #2	MAN #2	WOMAN #3	MAN #3	GIRL	BOY
			I'll talk to him				
							what's the big deal?
		Robbie what your grandfather told you is a lie a mean nasty terrible lie and you can never ever say it again is that clear?					
							okay I'll have an enchilada
(SHIFT) *(enters)*	**(SHIFT)** *(enters)* **ROBERT** don't listen to her, Robbie the enchiladas are terrible	**(SHIFT)**	**(SHIFT)**			**(SHIFT)**	**(SHIFT)**
			dad come on we're just trying to get through this meal				
	well you're gonna want his meal to get through his asshole						
			dad				*(laughs)*
ALICE Robert jesus						what'd he say? what's so funny? mom what'd he say?	
there are children at the table	what? it's true I had an enchilada here last time we came to visit and I was clogged up for a week an entire friggin week!	he said apple yes he did				 why's he laughing about apples?	no he didn't

WOMAN #1	MAN #1	WOMAN #2	MAN #2	WOMAN #3	MAN #3	GIRL	BOY
good god no one wants to hear about your clog		if you keep talking like that I'm gonna make you sit in the car					apples of the butt
							nuh uh
it's so nice to see you again		yes huh					
		oh you too					
you know what you need Nicky? a Cadillac Margarita!							
		thanks Alice but I've got wine				I'm gonna have a hamburger mom	
	I remember there being somewhere in the area better than this						
			well we wanted to take you to that place in the city but with the kids it's not so easy			I'm gonna have a hamburger	
		good just tell that to the server when she gets here					
maybe you can take us there tomorrow? you talk about it so much							
		(we work tomorrow)	we have to work I told you that				
		what do you say when we order?					
		and?				please	
		Robbie!					butthole
	maybe you could get off?						
			we can't you guys know this				what? grandpa said it
		Maddie sit up					

WOMAN #1	MAN #1	WOMAN #2	MAN #2	WOMAN #3	MAN #3	GIRL	BOY
	it's not every day we come to visit						
		then pull them down				but my socks itch	
			guys come on				
okay sorry (she peruses the menu) (long pause)	(he peruses the menu) (long pause)	(long pause)	(long pause)			(long pause)	(long pause) can I go to the game store?
						yeah! can I go too?	
							I wanna go by myself
							come on it's just right there
		I don't know					
			you're not buying any more games				
						can I go?	
							I know I just wanna look
		you just wanna look?					
						can I go?	
							I just wanna see what's new
			you can go if you bring Maddie				
oh let him go							I wanna go by myself!
			well that's the deal				
							that's so lame
		do you wanna go or not?					
							fine let's go
	hey Robbie						
							what?
	you forgot something						
							I did?
	yeah you dropped something under your chair						

WOMAN #1	MAN #1	WOMAN #2	MAN #2	WOMAN #3	MAN #3	GIRL	BOY
							no I didn't
	why don't you look?						
							(he looks under his chair. he finds a simply wrapped box.)
							whoa
							what's this?
	open it when you get home					what is it? do I have one? how come there's nothing under my chair? why didn't I forget something, Grandpa?	why can't I open it now?
you know Maddie's asking a very good question, Robert how come there's nothing for your granddaughter?		great just great look at her					
	I don't have anything for her just yet this one's for the boy Maddie no offense darling but I don't have anything for you		dad				*(he opens the box. it's an old watch.)* cool *(he puts it on his wrist.)*
			dad				
		(hey you think maybe your dad could consider Maddie sometimes?)				but will you next time?	
Robert	maybe						
			dad				
	I mean yes yes I will, Maddie and it'll heal the world it'll abolish prejudice are you happy?						
			hey				
the sarcasm always the sarcasm							
			don't screw around				

WOMAN #1	MAN #1	WOMAN #2	MAN #2	WOMAN #3	MAN #3	GIRL	BOY
							wow it's got a watch inside the watch
	oh lay off	Maddie why don't you and Robbie go to the game store okay?	these are my children				
…	…	…	…			(**MADDIE** cries. the others take in this sad sight.)	
see what you did? you see?	christ						
	Alice–	oh Maddie honey come here					
			dad apologize			no one ever has anything for me	
		that's not true					
Robert	why?						
	(sighs) darling …I…I'm sorry I didn't mean anything by it I just–						
			Maddie! take that back–! Maddie! come back here!			I HOPE YOU DIE!	
		(laughs)				(she becomes embarrassed by what she has said and runs off.)	
young lady!			(he turns to **NICOLE**) this isn't a joke				hey wait for me
							(he runs off with her.)
		I'm sorry but (laughs)					
Sam I hate to say it but we didn't drive nine hours for this kind of behavior you've gotta get that girl under control oh Robert hold on you	let's just figure out what we want to eat so we can order		I know mom I know				

WOMAN #1	MAN #1	WOMAN #2	MAN #2	WOMAN #3	MAN #3	GIRL	BOY
just ate a whole thing of chips!	can we order? oh		*(back to NICOLE)* what is wrong with you?				
		where…where did you people come from? *(laughs)*					
(SHIFT)	**(SHIFT)**	**(SHIFT)**	**(SHIFT)**	**(SHIFT)**			
(she continues to peruse the menu)	*(he continues to peruse the menu)*		*(at a separate table that is the same table)*				
				(enters) **JESSICA** hey Sam			
			oh hey Jess				
				where are the uh bambinos?			
			with Nicky's sister				
				oh yeah? what's Nicky up to?			
			my parents are in town so she's taken it upon herself to vanish *(drinks)*				
				(smiles) yeah parents are intense I mean I'm sure your parents are great but um you know what I mean			
			(smiles)	*(smiles)*			

WOMAN #1	MAN #1	WOMAN #2	MAN #2	WOMAN #3	MAN #3	GIRL	BOY
				but does she uh does she know we're all hanging out?			
			who?				
				Nicky			
			uh it's a work party				
				okay			
			(smiles, matter of fact) I'm allowed to have friends				
(SHIFT)	**(SHIFT)**	**(SHIFT)**	**(SHIFT)**	**(SHIFT)**	**(SHIFT)**	**(SHIFT)**	**(SHIFT)**
	and so they guy says "el barrio? lo siento señor! I thought you meant el baño!" *(laughs)*						
huh		that is funny very funny Sam? what do you wanna get?	*(laughs a little)*				
			I don't know				
		you wanna split something?					
			like what?				
you think the mole sauce has trans fats?							
	you've got to stop watching television						
			I kinda want shrimp				
			okay				
it's not make believe, Robert trans fats are a killer							
	well then let em kill you already						

WOMAN #1	MAN #1	WOMAN #2	MAN #2	WOMAN #3	MAN #3	GIRL	BOY
don't speak to me like that			dad come on				
	it's a joke!						
it's in poor taste							
	it's in perfectly good taste!						
Sam what would that counselor man say? would he say your father's brutishness is in good taste?		*(drinks)* uh how do you know about the counselor, Alice? (how does she know about the counselor?)	let's not talk about the counselor right now, okay mom?				
did I say something wrong?			(they asked what am I supposed to do lie to my parents?)				
	what's the matter? you don't like the guy? I thought you liked the guy	(yes!)					
		not really	he's great				
			you don't like the counselor?				
	now I don't want to run my mouth but you should know	no he's fine he's forget it why are we talking about this?					
and what are you gonna do? you're gonna run your mouth	(oh pipe down)						
	you should know that at this point in your marriage it is perfectly normal to be having problems with physical						

WOMAN #1	MAN #1	WOMAN #2	MAN #2	WOMAN #3	MAN #3	GIRL	BOY
	intimacy						
Robert			dad				
	now hold on						
	look I know you kids						
	love each other very						
	much but they don't						
	call it the seven year						
	rash for nothing						
itch							
itch	what?						
it's called the seven		oh my god					
year itch			twelve years				
			dad we've been				
			married twelve years				
	of course it is						
	what did I say?						
you said rash							
	well you know what?						
	it feels more like						
	a rash						
	I think rash is better						
(SHIFT)	**(SHIFT)**	**(SHIFT)**	**(SHIFT)**	**(SHIFT)**		**(SHIFT)**	**(SHIFT)**
						(runs in)	*(runs in)*
						MADDIE	**ROBBIE**
						mom dad!	
							dad!
						I need to tell you	
						something	she's lying
							don't listen to her
						Robbie pushed me	she's totally lying
							seriously don't listen
						yes he did	to her she's not telling
			guys			I was looking at the	the truth I would
		hey				princess movie and he	never do something
						told me you can see	like that! why would I
			calm down			the princess' boobs in	do that I love her she's
		you need to slow				this other movie where	my sister I love her
			what happened?			she does it with a	more than anything
						pirate who does it with	she's my sister why
	wohoho		did you push her?			other pirates and I said	would I do that

WOMAN #1	MAN #1	WOMAN #2	MAN #2	WOMAN #3	MAN #3	GIRL	BOY
		I can't understand				you're lying the princess wouldn't do that and he said no I'm not and so I said how would you know do you do it with pirates who do it with other pirates and then he pushed me	no
			well it sounds like				I didn't dad you have to believe me
		hey					
		we shouldn't have let them go					I didn't push you!
						he shoved me	
is she scraped? it looks like she's scraped!							see? she's already changing her story that means she's lying
		she's fine	cut it out listen to me				
are you sure?							
		yes they fight it's fine everything's fine					you're a compulsive liar and you're too dumb to even know what compulsive means
			hey! both of you calm down				
						I hate you, Robbie you're the devil and you have boobs	
							unlike you
						take it back	
							you told grandpa you wanted him to die

WOMAN #1	MAN #1	WOMAN #2	MAN #2	WOMAN #3	MAN #3	GIRL	BOY
		guys! hey! do you want to be grounded? cuz you keep acting like this that's exactly what's gonna happen				you just like him cuz he gives you stuff	
	ooooh watch out kids here comes big momma!						
	(laughs)						
		(she's livid, but tries with all her might not to respond)					
(pause)	*(pause)*	*(pause)*	*(pause)*			*(pause)*	*(pause)*
							I'm gonna go play video games across the street
						where?	
							at Lamppost Pizza
						I'm coming	
							no you're not
						I have quarters	
							fine
			(squeezes NICOLE's shoulder)			*(she goes)*	*(he goes)*
			(takes a drink)				
(SHIFT)	**(SHIFT)**	**(SHIFT)**	**(SHIFT)**	**(SHIFT)**	**(SHIFT)**	**(SHIFT)**	**(SHIFT)**
				(laughs)			
			—and so the guy says				

WOMAN #1	MAN #1	WOMAN #2	MAN #2	WOMAN #3	MAN #3	GIRL	BOY
			"el baño? lo siento señor I thought you said… EL BARRIO" *(laughs)* or uh maybe it's the other way around I don't know	*(laughs)* that's good			
			yeah				
				barrio that's funny			
			thanks yeah …Nicky thinks it's racist				
				well it is a little racist			
			sure a little yeah I guess				
				but that's what makes it funny I mean it's racist but it's not offensive or anything			
			"EL BARRIO!"				
				haha			
			no harm no foul right?				
				right			
				(smiles)			
			(smiles)				

WOMAN #1	MAN #1	WOMAN #2	MAN #2	WOMAN #3	MAN #3	GIRL	BOY
				lemme see your hand			
			why?				
				I wanna read your future			
			you're into that crap?				
				come on hand it over			
			seriously?				
				(she grabs his hands. studies them.)			
			what does it say?				
				hold on			
			well?				
				...I don't know			
			what do you mean you don't know?				
				I'm new at this okay?			
			talk about a tease *(laughs)*				
				(laughs)			
			(he lets go of her hand)				
				hey so I was gonna go to this show			
			oh yeah?				
				yeah these friends of mine they're supposed to be good			
			cool sounds like your friends are pretty cool				
				oh yeah big time ...you wanna tag along?			
			tag along? like go with you?				

WOMAN #1	MAN #1	WOMAN #2	MAN #2	WOMAN #3	MAN #3	GIRL	BOY
				yeah			
			oh				
			uh				
			(smiles)				
				you don't have to			
				(smiles)			
			I know I don't have to				
			I mean I want to but				
			uh				
		(drinks. she might absetmindedly pick some lint off his shirt. something domestic, common, none too intimate.)	*(smiles)*				
			uh				
			…I'm um				
			…I'm…married				
				yeah I know			
			…	…			
				what's that have to do with?			
			uh	wait			
				what did you think I was asking?			
(continues to peruse)	*(continues to peruse)*						
			(smiles. embarrassed.)				
			I didn't think you were				
			no				
			look Jess				
				it's a concert, Sam			
			I know				
				I'm not some slut			
			whoa hey				
			I didn't say you were	you're the one who started hanging out with me			
			sure	so don't start acting like I'm the one doing something inappropriate here			
			hey can we chill out?				

WOMAN #1	MAN #1	WOMAN #2	MAN #2	WOMAN #3	MAN #3	GIRL	BOY
			no one's doing anything				
				what did you think was happening?			
			(smiles) I I didn't think anything was happening				
				oh?			
			yeah				
				(a grin) nothing was happening? …nothing?			
			(nervous, excited by her interest) no what– was I supposed to think that?				
(SHIFT)	**(SHIFT)**	**(SHIFT)**	**(SHIFT)**	**(SHIFT)**			
				(exits)			
		we're ready to order!					
well I'm not!			hold on a sec, dad				
	come on we haven't got all night I'm about to eat your mother's head						
hey!							
			fine if you feel like you can't wait				
		that's exactly what I feel like					
(SHIFT)	**(SHIFT)**	**(SHIFT)**	**(SHIFT)**				

WOMAN #1	MAN #1	WOMAN #2	MAN #2	WOMAN #3	MAN #3	GIRL	BOY
(at the same table but not in the same scene as M#2 and W#2)	*(at the same table but not in the same scene as M#2 and W#2)*		…so…uh…I was thinking maybe we could find some time to get away just the two of us			*(she runs in. she sits at the table. colors. same table but not the same scene.)*	*(he runs in. he sits at the table. colors. same table but not the same scene.)*
		the two of us?					
			yeah				
		you hate vacations					
			I love vacations				
		all you did in Barcelona was watch TV					
		why?	ohhh				
			what?				
		why? why a vacation? why now?					
		`	I don't know I thought it'd be fun I thought it'd be				
		uh huh					
			we could have some time for just you and me the two of us and what?				
		I saw you					
		don't give me what					
			what are you talking about?				
		at the restaurant with that that girl					
			what girl?				
		oh fuck you what girl fuck you					
			I don't know what you think you saw but				
		with the jacket					

WOMAN #1	MAN #1	WOMAN #2	MAN #2	WOMAN #3	MAN #3	GIRL	BOY
		the cute little and the hands I saw her holding your hand I saw her whispering she's the one from work right?	okay hold on Nicole listen please listen				
		you had your hand on her thigh	Nicole				
		you are	hey I can explain I can				
		you are such an asshole fuck you fuck you I don't care let the world know what a fuckin' asshole you are	hey we're we're in public it was nothing honey it was hey we didn't even– I I did not act on the–				
		what? what were you so brave not to act on?	not that there was anything to act on– okay there were feelings there were feelings but feelings alone are				
		I'm taking the kids and we're going to my sister's	not– hey hey no my parents are coming				
		oh so I can just grin and bear it through another fuckin meal with that condescending fuckin asshole and his miserable wife	into town next week this is not the time to no so the kids can see their				

WOMAN #1	MAN #1	WOMAN #2	MAN #2	WOMAN #3	MAN #3	GIRL	BOY
			grandparents so they				
		oh the kids don't like your parents either they're pests your mother last year she sat them down and made them write birthday cards to your father cuz they forgot	that's not true that doesn't matter what matters is				
			well that's good they should remember his birthday he's thier grandfather				
		they're children	that doesn't mean they don't have an obliga-tion				
		you don't like him either					
			yes I have issues with my father but those issues don't mean that my children				
		look you've met someone I…	you don't–				
		I've sort of met someone					
		so let's just walk away and start over let's–	what? you what? who? who did you "meet"? Nicky? what is going on?				
		(near tears, guilt-ridden) I'm sorry, Sam	you can't do this				
		my sister's agreed to					

WOMAN #1	MAN #1	WOMAN #2	MAN #2	WOMAN #3	MAN #3	GIRL	BOY
		let us live with her	no				
		until I can find a job	no				
			Nicole				
			look at me				
		I've made up my					
		mind, Sam	come on				
			hey				
			look at me				
		no					
		no					
		I won't	listen				
		I	just listen				
		I'm miserable, Sam	Nicole				
		miserable!	Nicky				
		no	please				
		I will not–					
	(CLANG)						
	(unbeknownst to everyone else, **M#1** *(as* **ROBERT***) is served a big plate of food. it's heavy. it makes a big clang sound when it hits the table. the clang shakes the table. he begins to eat his food. everyone else at the table notices him eating. they stop what they're doing. they avert each other's eyes. no one looks at* **M#1**. *he doesn't care. he keeps eating. he takes his time. he leaves the table when he's finished.)*						
(SHIFT)	**(SHIFT)**	**(SHIFT)**	**(SHIFT)**			**(SHIFT)**	**(SHIFT)**
(long, long pause)	*(long, long pause)*	*(long, long pause)*	*(long, long pause)*			*(long, long pause)*	*(long, long pause)*

WOMAN #1	MAN #1	WOMAN #2	MAN #2	WOMAN #3	MAN #3	GIRL	BOY
		I'm sorry, Sam					
		I'm so sorry					
			(…he is very, very shaken)				
						what's wrong?	
							what's the matter?
(…as is she…)							
Robert…							
…oh my dear dear							
dear…							
		(she takes Sam's hand.)					
		I'm not going					
		anywhere, okay?					
		I am right here					
						dad?	
						I'm sorry	
						I didn't really want	
						grandpa to die	
						dad?	
						I take it back	
						I really liked grandpa	
		Maddie not now					
						grandma?	
						you know I didn't	
						mean to right?	
		why don't you kids					
		color, okay?					
		(she keeps her hand					
		on Sam's.)	*(he is staring off. not*				
			really noticing				
			Nicole's hand.)				

WOMAN #1	MAN #1	WOMAN #2	MAN #2	WOMAN #3	MAN #3	GIRL	BOY
						I didn't mean to I didn't mean to I didn't mean to I didn't **(MADDIE** runs off.)	
							hey wait for me **(ROBBIE** runs off.)
(SHIFT)	(SHIFT)	(SHIFT)	(SHIFT)	(SHIFT)	(SHIFT)	(SHIFT)	(SHIFT)
				(runs in) **MADDIE** mom dad is this true? are you seriously letting this happen?	*(runs in)* **ROBBIE** hey wait dad she is freaking out I just brought up the car thing casually and she went off on me		
		hey calm down guys we're in public	is what true?	with the car			
			yeah what's the problem?				
				oh my god why does Robbie get the Nissan tonight?			
		Maddie	he's got a student council meeting		I have a student council meeting		
				and you buy that?			
					what is this Nuremberg?		
				like you know what that is			
		honey		come on I have a thing tonight Jennifer's mom let her have the car and he's lying			
			Robbie do you or don't you have a student council				

WOMAN #1	MAN #1	WOMAN #2	MAN #2	WOMAN #3	MAN #3	GIRL	BOY
			meeting tonight?				
					yeah		
					I do		
					of course I do		
					I'm in student council		
					we have meetings		
				see?	why wouldn't I have a student council meeting?		
				on a Friday night?			
		guys come on give it a rest			it's a social meeting		
				oh okay a "social meeting"			
					there's a swimming pool there are parents		
				more like suppliers			
					shut up Maddie		
		watch your–	hey! Robbie! that's your sister!	see? he's an asshole I don't get why he gets to have the Nissan whenever he wants			
		it's not whenever he wants			I have meetings for my future		
				last time you had a meeting for your future you crashed the car			
					I didn't crash the car		
		(he crashed the Nissan?)		then what do you call it when your car runs into a fence?			

WOMAN #1	MAN #1	WOMAN #2	MAN #2	WOMAN #3	MAN #3	GIRL	BOY
			(a scratch he scratched it)	is that like how people park in the future?			
					I barely hit the fence		
		(I didn't know that)					
				you smashed the passenger side door			
			(it's not a big–)				
		Robbie you hit something with the Nissan?					
					no mom I just dented it a little		
				yeah sure my friends can't get in that way now they have to climb over me			
					more like climb on top of you		
				what?			
		(oh god I don't even wanna know)			*(gives his sister a knowing look.)*		
				oh okay hey you guys wanna hear *why* Robbie crashed the car?			
			Maddie cut it out				
				why?			
		your brother is taking the car tonight you get it tomorrow night that's that					
				but I'm not doing anything fun tomorrow night I'm			

WOMAN #1	MAN #1	WOMAN #2	MAN #2	WOMAN #3	MAN #3	GIRL	BOY
				doing something fun tonight Jennifer's mom let her go and Robbie's lying look at him he's a liar	*(victorious)* thanks guys gotta go *(gathers his stuff)*		
			this isn't about Robbie				
				that's a first			
			is the attitude really necessary? there's one car and two of you what are we supposed to do?				
					I'm gonna be late later Maddie *(he exits)*		
		be careful!		yeah great don't die k? cool I like you so much			
		(pause)	*(pause)* *(he turns to* **NICOLE**)	*(pause)* *(she seethes, having been left with her parents in a cheesy restaurant far away from her friends.)*			
			hey did they raise the price on this sampler platter?				
		huh that's a drag					
				(rolls her eyes. jiggles her leg. growls.)			
		(SHIFT)	**(SHIFT)**	**(SHIFT)**	**(SHIFT)**		

WOMAN #1	MAN #1	WOMAN #2	MAN #2	WOMAN #3	MAN #3	GIRL	BOY
				okay guys *(sighs. smiles. hopeful.)* so this is um this is Steven	*(enters)*		
		oh! hey Steven Maddie's told us so much about you		it's Madeleine, mom not Maddie …jesus			
					STEVEN it's really good to meet you, mrs.–		
		call me Nicole *(smiles, drinks)*					
			I'm Maddie's father Sam		it's so nice of you guys to take me out to dinner		
			what? I thought you were paying				
			(laughs)				
			ah, I'm just pulling your leg, Steve	his name's Steven			
			sorry I guess everyone's just growing up too fast for me		it's okay		
		(he's cute)					

WOMAN #1	MAN #1	WOMAN #2	MAN #2	WOMAN #3 (mom)	MAN #3	GIRL	BOY
			so what are your interests, Steven?				
					well		
					I'm really into music		
			a musician				
					kind of		
				Steven's really talented			
			oh yeah? what do you play?				
					guitar mostly		
					but I can also play		
					drums a little		
			cool				
			very cool				
			well it looks like you				
			have yourself a pretty				
			cool guy, Maddie				
				thanks	thanks		
		how did you guys meet?					
				at school	at a party		
				a party at school			
				for Spanish			
				we're in Spanish			
				together			
				for Cindo de Mayo			
			well I met Maddie's				
			mother while she was				
			waitressing				
		Sam			oh		
			it's true!		cool		
			we weren't much older				
			than you two				

WOMAN #1	MAN #1	WOMAN #2	MAN #2	WOMAN #3	MAN #3	GIRL	BOY
			you kids should have seen her				
			she was gorgeous				
			and I went right up to her and lemme tell you, Maddie				
			your mother wasn't exactly looking to settle down				
			I mean the first date alone was *(laughs)*				
		that's not really how it happened	well–				
		at all					
		Maddie don't listen to this					
		Sam		okay we don't need to hear about how you like conquered mom			
		please	alright alright				
			so Cinco de Mayo huh? are you uh…Latino, Steven?				
					um		
					I'm adopted so I don't really know but I sort of doubt it		
			you know my dad used to tell this joke about Latinos				
			…it's not offensive but it's a little racy				
		Sam			dad		
			okay okay				
			(makes a whip sound as if he's fighting off lions. laughs.)				
			well despite what these ladies might tell you my dad was quite the comedian				

WOMAN #1	MAN #1	WOMAN #2	MAN #2	WOMAN #3	MAN #3	GIRL	BOY
					wow I uh I can't wait to meet him		
			that's nice of you to say but my dad passed away a long time ago				
					oh I'm sorry		
			it was a long time ago				
					still that really um sucks		
			(smiles) yeah well we'll all get there someday				
			what?	dad			
				you're being morbid			
			who's being morbid? death's a part of life am I right Steve?				
		(SHIFT)	**(SHIFT)**	**(SHIFT)**	**(SHIFT)**		
			then who's Steven?	his name's Marcus, dad			
				that was– what is wrong with you?!			
		where are your parents from, Marcus?			**MARCUS** Ohio		

WOMAN #1	MAN #1	WOMAN #2	MAN #2	WOMAN #3	MAN #3	GIRL	BOY
			Buckeyes				
					okay		
		(SHIFT)	(SHIFT)	(SHIFT)	(SHIFT)		
				Jeremy doesn't like football			
			who doesn't like football?				
				he plays tennis			
			oh yeah?				
				Jeremy's really talented, dad			
			what position?				
					JEREMY um there's kinda like only one position		
			mm well what should we have to eat? anyone want an appetizer?				
		don't listen to him					
		(he's cute)					
				(mom)			
			you want calamari?				
					oh I'm allergic sorry		
			to calamari?				
					to shellfish		
			then why can't you eat calamari?				
		(laughs)	is calamari a shellfish?				
				yes			
		oh Sam	excuse me				

WOMAN #1	MAN #1	WOMAN #2	MAN #2	WOMAN #3	MAN #3	GIRL	BOY
			excuse me!				
			am I talking to you?				
		hey don't talk to me	no				
		like that	I'm talking to uh				
		how dare you	uh	Patrick			
			Patrick right	oh my god			
		(SHIFT)	**(SHIFT)**	**(SHIFT)**	**(SHIFT)**		
		don't talk to me that	now Patrick				
		way	I thought calamari was				
			a a a		**PATRICK**		
		Sam	octopus	it's squid	it is but		
			okay squid but I don't				
			see what a squid has to				
			do with a clam or an				
		Sam	oyster or				
			what?				
		apologize		stop			
			for what?	please			
		first of all for your		stop			
		tone		we're in public			
			tone what tone?	oh my god			
		the way you spoke to		can't you guys be			
		me and Maddie was		normal for like			
		totally disrespectful		one meal?			
			you were mocking me	I knew this would			
		we were not mocking	both of you were	happen			
		you	mocking me and I'm	this always happens			
			supposed to respond	this was a bad idea I'm			
		Sam	in a respectful way	sorry I'm really sorry			
			when I'm shown little	they're being like this			
			to no respect myself?	but it's not okay			
		we weren't the ones		they're always like this			
		being disrespectful					
			then what do you call				
			that "oh Sam" with	maybe we should go			
			the little laugh?				
			if that's not mocking	we're going			
			then I don't know				
			what is				
		go?	wait wait did she				

WOMAN #1	MAN #1	WOMAN #2	MAN #2	WOMAN #3	MAN #3	GIRL	BOY
		what do you mean go?					
			you can't go		it was really nice meeting you guys		
				I mean me and Patrick are getting the hell away from this whole dysfunctional situation			
		dysfunctional?			I think since we're going I should really pay you guys for my meal		
		you think this is dysfunctional? god you're spoiled you know that?	no no Patrick	yeah dysfunctional	**MICHAEL** my name's Michael		
		(SHIFT)	**(SHIFT)**	**(SHIFT)**	**(SHIFT)**		
		you don't know a thing about dysfunction just take a look at the world look at all the terrible things happening in the world and tell me that this this is dysfunctional if anything you should feel blessed	right right right Michael you're not gonna pay okay? this is on us no no thank you but no		no please just lemme give you guys a little		
				oh yeah this is good you're not dysfunctional cuz there's like apartheid or something happening in some impoverished nation	it's okay my parents gave me some money		
			well that is certainly generous of them but we've got it covered	blessed? wow blessed okay			
		yeah get sarcastic that helps					
			it is very nice to meet you and I want to				

WOMAN #1	MAN #1	WOMAN #2	MAN #2	WOMAN #3	MAN #3	GIRL	BOY
			apologize for the way my daughter is behaving but		um okay		
				me? why are you apologizing for me? you're the one acting like a freak			
			a freak okay				
		Sam she's right you were not–					
			why don't you just order another drink?				
		what?					
			my mother's right you're more fun when you're drunk				
		(horrible pause)	*(horrible pause)*	*(horrible pause)*	*(horrible pause)*		
		(she is rattled)	*(he is embarrassed)* hey ah Nicky I'm sorry I didn't–				
		don't					
				seriously mom I can't believe you let him talk to you like this after what he did to you			
		Maddie					
			after what I did? what did I do?				
		(pause)	*(pause)*	*(pause)*	*(pause)*		
			Nicole? what did I do?				

WOMAN #1	MAN #1	WOMAN #2	MAN #2	WOMAN #3	MAN #3	GIRL	BOY
		Sam	you wanna fill me in here?	I'm sorry mom I didn't mean to mom I didn't mean to *(she goes)*	*(he goes)*		
		Sam					
			you wanna fill me in here on what *I* did?				
			(he slams the table with his palm)				
		(SHIFT)	**(SHIFT)**	**(SHIFT)**	**(SHIFT)**		
					(enters) **ROBBIE** hey mom dad		
		hey Robbie					
					um well		
				(enters, bright and cheery) **STEPHANIE** on my god hiii!	this is Stephanie		
		(and everyone stands up to shake hands) oh hey Stephanie! I'm Nicole we've heard so much about you					
				it's so nice to meet you guys			
			Stephanie? what happened to Marissa? *(laughs)*		dad		

WOMAN #1	MAN #1	WOMAN #2	MAN #2	WOMAN #3	MAN #3	GIRL	BOY
			I'm just pulling your leg Steph Marissa doesn't exist well at least not to my knowledge maybe Robbie's got a secret Marissa under the table watch out for this one		Robert my name's		
			(laughs)				
			oh I'm just having some fun		dad		
					it's not funny		
			call me Sam	thanks, Mr.–			
				thank you so much Sam			
			(hey way to go Robster) *(sizzle sound)*		(dad)		
(SHIFT)		**(SHIFT)**	**(SHIFT)**	**(SHIFT)**	**(SHIFT)**		
(enters.)							
ALICE							
I want a picture! hello? picture time!							
				mom	grandma		
oh shut up							
I want Robbie and his new girlfriend for my wallet							
saaaay nacho!							

WOMAN #1	MAN #1	WOMAN #2	MAN #2	WOMAN #3	MAN #3	GIRL	BOY
				nacho	nacho		
(SHIFT)		**(SHIFT)**	**(SHIFT)**	**(SHIFT)**	**(SHIFT)**		
		oh I like her, Robbie I like her a lot					
					yeah me too		
you know girls these day lack poise they lack class but Stephanie that is a very classy young lady					okay		
		I don't usually like "girly" girls but that Steph she is something else *(laughs)*					
					cool		
absolutely adorable							
					thank you		
		just don't fuck it up okay? men tend to fuck things up for themselves especially when they're happy					
					right		
your mother's right							
					yeah		
		god I hope you're using condoms you're using condoms right? sorry I'm sorry but I have to ask					
					mom		
					or not		
(SHIFT)		**(SHIFT)**	**(SHIFT)**	**(SHIFT)**	**(SHIFT)**		

WOMAN #1	MAN #1	WOMAN #2	MAN #2	WOMAN #3	MAN #3	GIRL	BOY
			so what's up?		(ROBBIE *adjust his wrist watch nervously*) um so what do you think of her, dad? I mean really		
			Stephanie? she's great she's a very nice girl				
			and well she's young		and?		
			you're young too, Robbie		she's just two years younger than me		
			all I'm saying is now is maybe not the time to be settling down		you think everyone who's not old is young I'm very professional for my age		
			no I just think you should play the field a little I mean let's be honest Robbie you met this girl in high school		well when's the time? when you say so? I've got plans dad I've got ambitions

play the field? uh wow | | |
| | | | restaurant we met at a–

nothing there's | | and you met mom at a bar what's wrong with high school? | | |

WOMAN #1	MAN #1	WOMAN #2	MAN #2	WOMAN #3	MAN #3	GIRL	BOY
			nothing wrong with it				
			it's just–				
					I love her		
			you–?				
			okay				
			sure				
			you love her				
			and that's				
			that is real				
			to you				
			right now				
			at this age		yeah		
			but		it is		
					no at any age		
			sure	**(SHIFT)**	it's real		
			of course sure	*(she clinks a glass)*	this is what I want		
			but				
				excuse me!			
			Robbie	hi!			
				excuse me!			
			(SHIFT)	um hi	**(SHIFT)**		
				so			
				Robbie and I have a			
				little announcement			
			announcement?				
					yeah		
				um			
				you wanna?			
					go ahead		
				okayokayokay…			
				WE'RE ENGAGED!			
how wonderful!		oh honey!		thanks			
how absolutely		that's great!	wow that is very…	thank you			
wonderful!		that's so great!	wow			*(and the drinks start flowing…)*	

WOMAN #1	MAN #1	WOMAN #2	MAN #2	WOMAN #3	MAN #3	GIRL	BOY
				(she runs over to the ladies)			
		(hugs her)					
		welcome					
		welcome to the family!					
a wedding!				thanks			
I love weddings!				um			
				mom			
		mom?	hey I uh thought we	is that okay?			
		wow!	were gonna talk about	can I call you mom?			
		I guess I kinda am	this some more, buddy				
		yeah go for it!			why?		
					I've made up my mind		
			of course you have				
			I just want you to				
			know that I'm always				
			here to help you make				
			your own decisions				
					dad		
					I'm getting married		
		oh I love this girl					
		don't you love this girl,	I know I know				
		Sam?					
			she's very nice				
					she's the love of my life		
		when's the wedding?					
				we don't know yet			
				but we're thinking			
				maybe Valentine's Day			
Valentine's Day!		wow!					
			that is definitely a				
			romantic day				

WOMAN #1	MAN #1	WOMAN #2	MAN #2	WOMAN #3	MAN #3	GIRL	BOY
				kissed	yeah it's the first day we uh kissed		
do you have a dress?							
				not yet			
		oh god you should've seen mine I don't know what I was thinking					
when you order the cake don't forget that I'm allergic to walnuts and marzipan							
					(dad can you please say something?)		
			(of course yeah) **(SAM** *stands, toasts)* …uh Stephanie honey hey congratulations				
				(she practically tackles **SAM** *with a hug.)* oh my god thank you thank you so much *(she is duddenly crying)*			
			are are you okay?				
				yeah it's just I'm so happy			
			and your dad's footing the bill for this, right? it's a joke I'm joking TRADITION! welcome to the family!				
		Sam			dad		

WOMAN #1	MAN #1	WOMAN #2	MAN #2	WOMAN #3	MAN #3	GIRL	BOY
(SHIFT)	(SHIFT)	(SHIFT)	(SHIFT)	(SHIFT)	(SHIFT)		
	(enters w/cigar)						
	JACK hey who let all these handsome people in here? huh?						
				oh hey guys everyone this is my dad Jack			
		(everyone gets up to shake Jack's hand)					
			hey Jack! Sam				
	great to meet you Sam great to meet you						
I'm Alice							
	you must be Robbie's mother						
(laughs) grandmother actually							
	get out! with that figure?						
oh! *(laughs)*	*(laughs)*				he's good he's very good		
		hi Jack I'm Nicole Robbie's mom					
	an absolute pleasure c'mere!						

WOMAN #1	MAN #1	WOMAN #2	MAN #2	WOMAN #3	MAN #3	GIRL	BOY
	(he turns his handshake with Nicole into a sweet little twirl)						
		whoa ha ha!					
	heck of a boy you raised						
		thank you					
			thanks Jack				
	if I may say one little thing to the love birds?						
		of course	sure				
	now Steph and I went through a lot						
	what with everything between me and her mother						
	so forgive me for getting sentimental for a moment						
	but if I've learned anything kids, it's this:						
	love is not California						
	with love there's a lot of storms and hail and sleet						
	we all know something about sleet around here now don't we?						
		(knowing laughs at the table)					
	but you know what? it passes it might not seem like it but it passes and it makes						

WOMAN #1	MAN #1	WOMAN #2	MAN #2	WOMAN #3	MAN #3	GIRL	BOY
	everything else a hell of a lot more beautiful for having braved the stuff so please whatever you do Steph? Robbie? you hearing this? whatever you do…						
	don't move to California!						
(laughs)	it's very far away and I can't stand the place!	*(laughs)*	*(laughs)*	*(laughs)*	*(laughs)*	*(laughs)*	
				we won't, daddy			
					you got it, Jack		
	okay enough of that nonsense let's have a party!						
				(and the family dance dance dances. stomping and hollering with a visceral celebration of love and life.) **(SAM** and **NICOLE** *look on with a kind of bewildered wonder, then begin to dance with one another. and just as quickly as the dance began it's over.)*			
(SHIFT)	**(SHIFT)**	**(SHIFT)**	**(SHIFT)**	**(SHIFT)**	**(SHIFT)**		
(sighs)	*(sighs)*	*(sighs)* oh what an awesome wedding!	*(sighs)*	*(sighs)*	*(sighs)* *(drinks, stumbles a little)*		
		can you?		can you believe this? *(Castillian voice)* mmm yes yes I can *(they kiss)*			
where's Maddie run off to? I saw her with some man? has anyone	god she's beautiful						

WOMAN #1	MAN #1	WOMAN #2	MAN #2	WOMAN #3	MAN #3	GIRL	BOY
seen Maddie?	isn't my little girl beautiful?						
my wedding night was something else let me tell you I had only been with one man before Robert one! oh but thank god thank god for that				kinda loud honey	*(clinks a glass aggressively, stands. drunk.)* I want to thank my incredible family mom: you're awesome dad: thanks thanks for everything I mean I know you don't like condone our marriage or anything but it's fine it's a little *(gesture)* but it's fine		
			I never said that				
			Stephanie honey you have to know I never said anything like that I adore you I totally adore you	I think my husband's had a little too much fun *(takes the drink)*			
					hey!		
				what?			
					give it back		
				no way			
					I love you		
				I love you too			

WOMAN #1	MAN #1	WOMAN #2	MAN #2	WOMAN #3	MAN #3	GIRL	BOY
					so can I have it back now or what?		
		(pretty damn drunk) have another drink, Steph!		oh I'm not drinking			
		(drinks) you're not drinking? you just got married!					
				I know but I really shouldn't			
(pretty damn drunk) oh pull the cork out of your ass and drink up! *(laughs)*							
				thanks yeah I would guys I would but I feel I feel a little sick oh…			
(SHIFT)	**(SHIFT)**	**(SHIFT)**	**(SHIFT)**	**(SHIFT)**	**(SHIFT)**	**(SHIFT)**	
						(enters)	
					(he clinks a glass) hey guys! guys! everyone! hey! I wanna introduce you… to Jacquelyn		
ooooooooooh	heeeeey-oooo		*(laughs and claps)*				
		oh my god she's gorgeous she's oh Robbie Stephanie she's perfect	that's my boy! *(laughs)* wow wow		isn't she?		
	you're damn right	she's just perfect					

WOMAN #1	MAN #1	WOMAN #2	MAN #2	WOMAN #3	MAN #3	GIRL	BOY
			say hello Jackie			**JACKIE** hello	
who wants another Cadillac Margarita?! yeah I invented this mother fucker!	oooh would you look at her? look at those cheeks	ooooooooooh	aaahhhhhhhh she's cute she is very cute you're a doll, Jackie		yeah she's pretty much the best		
aaaaaahhhh	*(laughs)*	oooooh!	what a miracle			hello!	
(drunker)							
picture time! picture time!			mom		grandma		
oh shut up							
saaay nacho!	nacho	nacho	nacho	nacho	nacho	nacho	
(SHIFT)	**(SHIFT)**	**(SHIFT)**	**(SHIFT)**	**(SHIFT)**	**(SHIFT)**	**(SHIFT)**	
			(he clinks a glass) so I've heard a rumor a teeny tiny rumor that I'm… GONNA HAVE A GRANDSON!				
	(whistle and applause)	what? oh that's incredible! that's so			it's true		
ooooooh! a picture! we need to take a			a boy! a baby boy!		yeah we're expecting again yeah isn't that great?	yep yep thanks ha ha	

WOMAN #1	MAN #1	WOMAN #2	MAN #2	WOMAN #3	MAN #3	GIRL	BOY
picture!	that's my Steph that's my little Steph	it's so great!				dad	
where's my camera? has anyone seen my camera?	hey lemme buy you a drink, Alice	when are you due?	WOW	pretty soon	yeah sweetie?		
oh for the love of god, Jack	(laughs) you're a spitfire you know that?	you've got to be thrilled		I am we both are we're really excited	that's right yes your brother's gonna be very nice	is he gonna be nice?	
		I am I am so happy for you	hey-ooooooo! ha ha ha ha!	(she holds **ROBBIE**'s hand)	of course	promise?	
							<u>**CLANG**</u> (the boy is served a plate of chicken fingers. the plate is heavy. it makes a big clang sound when it hits the table. everyone stops what they're doing. they avoid eye contact. this will take the boy a long time to eat. he exits when he's finished.)
(long pause)	(long pause) damn it	(long pause)	(long pause)	(long pause)	(long pause)	(long pause)	(long pause)

WOMAN #1	MAN #1	WOMAN #2	MAN #2	WOMAN #3	MAN #3	GIRL	BOY
		I'm sorry					
	god damn it						
			did they tell you what happened?				
					dad		
		I'm so sorry			*(he drinks)*		
				(sobs and runs off)			

(ALICE *is shaken, as if reliving her husband's death all over again*)

ALICE
when my husband
died, I went to this man
downtown who worked
in this little room with
pastels on the walls
and I'd sit in a chair
and talk to him only I
don't remember myself
talking
I only knew that I had
talked because of the
bill I got in the mail
every month
and I wish I could
remember what I said
I hope I didn't tell him
anything terrible about
your father cuz I loved
him
yes sometimes Robert
was unkind to me
but at the core of him
was a good person

WOMAN #1	MAN #1	WOMAN #2	MAN #2	WOMAN #3	MAN #3	GIRL	BOY
one of the best people the world has ever known							
so what I've started doing is I've begun to write letters							
and these letters are addressed to my husband and I talk to him							
and I tell him how much I miss him I tell him what's happening in your lives and the baseball scores and the state of the yard and I tell him how glad I'll be to see him							
and I've told him how he has a great grandchild on his way to meet him there and how though none of us ever met him he is a very curious person a very kind person and they will have lots to talk about							
oh my husband will have lots to tell your son							
so don't be sad							
don't be sad							
I was sad for a long time but if you just get a little envelope and talk to him it'll make you feel so much better why just try now just try writing to him now just write right here say hello							

WOMAN #1	MAN #1	WOMAN #2	MAN #2	WOMAN #3	MAN #3	GIRL	BOY
just say hello tell him you love him right now right this moment just say hello go on go on go on							
<u>CLANG</u> (**ALICE** *is served a big plate of food. she eats and eats. she exits when she's finished.*)							
(long pause)							
(SHIFT)	*(SHIFT)*	*(SHIFT)*	*(SHIFT)*	*(SHIFT)*	*(SHIFT)*	*(SHIFT)*	*(SHIFT)*
		*(she takes **SAM**'s hand)*	*(he is deeply shaken. he stares blankly.)*	*(enters)* **MADDIE** it's okay dad it's gonna be okay			
		NICOLE we're so glad you made it, Maddie					
				thanks mom yeah they let me take my finals early so			
	JACK she was a great woman of course I didn't know her as long or as well as the rest of you but she was a real spitfire and sure sure well who wants a drink?	thank you Jack					
		I'll take one					

WOMAN #1	MAN #1	WOMAN #2	MAN #2	WOMAN #3	MAN #3	GIRL	BOY
that's the spirit! what'll you have?							
		uh how about a Cadillac Margarita? *(laughs)*					
	alright! now lemme track down that server *(exits)*		*(smiles a little)*	dad if you need anything seriously dad			
		I'm not going anywhere you understand me? I'm right here I'm here for you, Sam					
			you know mom used to say you never really understand how alone you are until you lose em both				
		(SHIFT) *(exits)*	**(SHIFT)**		**(SHIFT)** **ROBBIE** hey sorry I can't be at the funeral, dad (yeah I'll) hang on dad (yeah whiskey thanks) dad you there? *(checks his watch)* it's just my plane's about to leave for Orlando and (thanks thanks) *(drinks)*		

WOMAN #1	MAN #1	WOMAN #2	MAN #2	WOMAN #3	MAN #3	GIRL	BOY
			Orlando? what's in Orlando?		you there?		
			I'm here				
					yeah sorry I requested the time but you know the company's in a bit of a bind, Steph's business is blowing up, and Jackie's busy with her schooling and (hey you know what can I get this neat? …NEAT?) dad? you there?		
	SAM I'm here						
			ROBBIE hey look dad I gotta go				
	…Orlando						
			I'd be there if I could				
	yeah okay						
			it's just…too much				
	well lemme know if you change your mind, buddy						
			(checks his watch) it's just a little too much *(drinks)*				

WOMAN #1	MAN #1	WOMAN #2	MAN #2	WOMAN #3	MAN #3	GIRL	BOY
(SHIFT)		(SHIFT)					
(NICOLE *alone. she waits. peruses the menu.*)							
		(enters)					
		MADDIE					
NICOLE		hey mom					
there you are							
		sorry I'm late					
it's okay Maddie sit down							
		thanks um					
		thanks for meeting me					
		I know it's last minute					
it's not a problem		*(she sits)*					
so what's up?							
		(hopeful)					
		it's not well					
		okay um					
		I'm pregnant!					
what?							
Maddie holy shit		yeah					
Maddie							
with who?							
I didn't		his name's Darius					
I didn't know you		it just					
were seeing anyone		just sorta happened					
Darius?							
		yeah					
		for like a year now					
a year?							
okay							

WOMAN #1	MAN #1	WOMAN #2	MAN #2	WOMAN #3	MAN #3	GIRL	BOY
so what's what's the story with Darius?							
		well he's a painter					
wow							
		he's really talented, mom					
so I mean is that it? have you covered I don't know every genre? I mean there was that video artist, then there was that string of musicians, that dancer that actor, you had that chiropractor for a while, not sure that counts as an artist but		painting is not a genre it's a form of visual okay

okay it's not like that, mom

we're in love, mom, okay? we're in love | | | | | |
| oh lighten up when did you get so serious? | | | | | | | |
| | | uh hello | | | | | |
| Maddie honey trust me I used to fall for these types of guys all the time these scrappy needy narcissistic…oh you know I mean the guy I was dating before I met your father was– well he was a freak but he was a sexy freak extremely attentive | | types? what types? scrappy?

uh no I don't

so now Darius is a freak? | | | | | |

WOMAN #1	MAN #1	WOMAN #2	MAN #2	WOMAN #3	MAN #3	GIRL	BOY
so I get it I get the thing you're going through		okay you haven't even met him I'm not going through anything I'm in love					
remember Steven? Jeremy? uh uh Marcus?							
		yeah I've dated a bunch of guys so what?					
are you and Dario							
		Darius					
right are you and he planning to get married or?							
		married?! oh my god who are you? you and dad barely had a wedding!					
forget it forget I said anything							
(small pause) alright well you know what you get older and you start to see things a little differently		*(small pause)*					
		okay so now I have to be like Robbie and his perky little wife and everyone else in this fucking wasteland yeah right					
this isn't about Robbie							
		that's a first					

WOMAN #1	MAN #1	WOMAN #2	MAN #2	WOMAN #3	MAN #3	GIRL	BOY
		…and for the record that wedding sucked it was super cheesy					
oh get over it							
		hey why don't you get a drink?					
I stopped drinking							
		oh really?					
yes							
		when?					
when that alcoholic grandmother of yours finally kicked the bucket							
(laughs)		*(laughs)*					
wow Maddie another grandchild well I'm you know what? I'm ecstatic							
		really?					
of course! you're my baby girl! now come here! *(she hugs* **MADDIE***)*							
		thanks mom					
…just don't fuck it up okay?							

WOMAN #1	MAN #1	WOMAN #2	MAN #2	WOMAN #3	MAN #3	GIRL	BOY
(SHIFT)	**(SHIFT)**	**(SHIFT)**	**(SHIFT)**			**(SHIFT)**	
NICOLE	**SAM**	**MADDIE**	**ROBBIE**			**JACKIE**	
(sings) happy happy birthday from all of us to you happy happy birthday we're all so proud of you happy happy birthday from all of us to you happy happy birthday may all your dreams come true happy birthday SAAAAAAAAM *(claps)*	*(delighted)* you've gotta be kidding	*(sings)* happy happy birthday from all of us to you happy happy birthday we're all so proud of you we're all so proud of from all of us to you happy happy birthday may all your dreams come true happy birthday SAAAAAAAAM *(whistles)*	*(sings)* happy happy birthday from all of us to you happy happy birthday we're all so proud of you we're all so proud of from all of us to you happy happy birthday may all your dreams come true happy birthday SAAAAAAAAM *(claps)*			*(sings)* happy happy birthday from all of us to you happy happy birthday we're all so proud of you we're all so proud of from all of us to you happy happy birthday may all your dreams come true happy birthday GRAAANDPAAA *(jumps a little)*	
	(laughs. he might take a picture.) now who hatched this little scheme?	*(everyone is in a very jovial mood)*	I'm afraid that's classified information				
Jackie how could you?! I couldn't help myself …happy birthday Sam *(she kisses him)*	Nicky? *(big smile)* well there's nothing that works up the appetite quite like a public seruhm uh serum oh Nicky what is that word?	*(hugs)* happy birthday, daddy	*(hugs)* we love you, dad			GRANDMA!	

WOMAN #1	MAN #1	WOMAN #2	MAN #2	WOMAN #3	MAN #3	GIRL	BOY
serenade!							
(laughs)	(smiles)	(laughs)	(laughs)				
	right right serenade!						
	...so uh						
	who wants an						
	appetizer?						
			bring it on				
	how about calamari?						
uh							
your daughter's							
pregnant, Sam							
	so?						
	she's not allowed to						
	eat calamari?						
Sam–		dad–					
	I thought pregnant						
	women ate everything						
			dad, it's a shellfish				
	I've seen em at the						
	aquarium and I don't						
when have you ever	buy it for a second						
been to an aquarium?			well I hate to break it				
			to you but science has				
			a system a				
			classification system–				
	Robbie, it's cooked!						
	how can it be bad for						
	her if it's cooked?	it's okay dad I'm just					
		being careful					
	(warm)						
	there's being careful						
	and then there's being		(drinks)				
	crazy pants		hey it's tricky stuff			dad	
	and I think you're		you know Steph and I				
	being a little crazy		went through the same			daddy	
	pants		thing with				
						hey daddy	
			hold on dad				

WOMAN #1	MAN #1	WOMAN #2	MAN #2	WOMAN #3	MAN #3	GIRL	BOY
			what's up Jackie?				
						can I get a corndog?	
			a corndog?				
						yeah they're the best	
no way							
	oh Nicole let her have the corndog						
now Jackie what do you think your mom'll say when she finds out we let you have a corndog?							
						um ...did you get me one?	
(laughs)	(laughs)	(laughs)	(laughs)				
somehow I don't think so							
	she's a doll I always said she was a doll		no no mommy will not be happy with daddy if she comes back from her business trip and finds her little girl hopped up on peservatives no you'll get something else			she would! dad! I'll only have a little I promise!	
	so how's work, stranger?						
		dad					
			uh Steph's new venture's taking off so				
	no I mean your work–						
			you know ...same old same old				
		uh hello earth to dad	(drinks)				

WOMAN #1	MAN #1	WOMAN #2	MAN #2	WOMAN #3	MAN #3	GIRL	BOY
	I'm talking to your brother						
		well I wanna give you your birthday present					
	can it wait?						
		no					
	(closes his eyes. opens his hands. playful.) alright lay it on me						
		(takes his hand) I have decided to name him after you					
	who? what are you talking about?						
what do you think she's talking about, Sam?		uh him my baby oh my god					
	it's a boy?						
		yeah					
	and you're naming him after me?						
		yes					
	well hey that's pretty cool! *(laughs)*						
(SHIFT)	**(SHIFT)**	**(SHIFT)**	**(SHIFT)**			**(SHIFT)**	**(SHIFT)**
							(enters)

WOMAN #1	MAN #1	WOMAN #2	MAN #2	WOMAN #3	MAN #3	GIRL	BOY SAMMY
							MEEERRRRY EX– MAS!
							MERRRRRY EX– MAS!
							(he does a hyperactive ninja move)
well look who it is!							
	Sammy's back!						
		Sammy honey sit down next to your cousin the food's gonna be coming out soon					
	(kinda racist accent) hoooo beware the Sammy-rai! *(laughs)*						
		a little racist, dad					
very funny, Sam							
							HO HO HO!
						ow! don't yell in my ear	
							HI-YA!
						dad make him stop	
			Maddie? your son can you get him to?				
		…Sammy? how many times do I have to tell you? leave your cousin alone					
		now say you're sorry					
							fine
							sorry Jackie
							(he kisses her cheek)
		buddy–					

WOMAN #1	MAN #1	WOMAN #2	MAN #2	WOMAN #3	MAN #3	GIRL	BOY
						ew! don't!	
	(laughs)						what?
		come on dad you're just encouraging him					I'm saying sorry!
	the kid's funny					you got my cheek wet	
	so what were you up to out there, *(racist)* Sammy-rai?						
							I was making a snowman...WITH TITS
well okay then	*(laughs)* oh yeah? what size were her snow cones? huh?	you what? no	*(weird look)*				yeah!
Sam grow up he doesn't even know what he's saying	*(laughs)*						*(laughs)*
	come on Nicky it's a joke!						then a dog came over and peed on it so it looked like the snowman peed while standing up but girls don't pee standing up only boys do SO I PUNCHED HER TITS OFF!
alright where's he getting this stuff?		god okay no don't don't do that again okay? you have to be nice to girls even snowman girls	he's got an imagination I'll give him that				HI-YAH!

WOMAN #1	MAN #1	WOMAN #2	MAN #2	WOMAN #3	MAN #3	GIRL	BOY
							why?
		well for starters because your mother's a girl and you wanna be nice to me don't you?					
							sometimes
hey!		Sammy!					
			you know Mad I know a guy like a child behavioral guy–				
		thanks but no thanks Rob					
			are you sure?				
							(he does something ridiculous) YAH YAH YAH
you know what! let's do some presents!							
		I thought we weren't doing Christmas tonight					
well now we're doing Christmas							
							PREEEESENTS!
		come on guys I didn't know this was happening I haven't done my shopping				you're loud in my ear again!	
(she tries to slow things down)							

WOMAN #1	MAN #1	WOMAN #2	MAN #2	WOMAN #3	MAN #3	GIRL	BOY
Jackie darling... since you have been so well behaved you get to go first! *(presents a box)*							
						(she opens it. inside is a compass on a necklace.)	
						I don't know what it is	
it can take you wherever you want to go							
						how's it do that?	
				it's a compass, honey see those are magnets and–			
yep! anywhere! you can go anywhere!						and I can go anywhere with a compass?	
				it's a metaphor now what do you say to Grandma Nicky?			
							(where's mine? where's my present?)
						thank you	
you're very welcome		*(Sammy)*					
						how do you turn it on?	*(what? I wanna go next)*
it's always on it doesn't need to turn on		*(be patient)*					
						but how's it take me places?	
		hey					SHUT UP JACKIE!

WOMAN #1	MAN #1	WOMAN #2	MAN #2	WOMAN #3	MAN #3	GIRL	BOY
		whoa Sammy				you're being rude!	
			hold on				well you're being a spoiled little brat
			none of this hey			I am not!	
							that's what my mom says
		no no I don't know where he got that	what did you? Maddie seriously? did you tell him that?			take it back	
			(to SAM) let me handle it, dad				
							TWAT TWAT TWAT!
now where the hell did he learn that?		Sammy! oh my god get over here!				daddy!	
							I heard you say it to dad!
			say what? what did he say?				
	the T word						
		nothing he didn't– see? he didn't say anything					nothing
	(you know maybe your sister could watch him next time we go out)						I was just making fun
(my sister's not a babysitter, Sam)							
	(can't hurt to ask)		they're cousins he needs to learn to respect his cousin				
		I'm sorry, Rob really					

WOMAN #1	MAN #1	WOMAN #2	MAN #2	WOMAN #3	MAN #3	GIRL	BOY
		I don't know where he got that *(she gives* **SAMMY** *a look)*					
							*(***SAMMY** *grins at his mom, then hides it)*
		(sternly whispers to her son) shut…up…					
(SHIFT)	**(SHIFT)**	**(SHIFT)**	**(SHIFT)**			**(SHIFT)**	**(SHIFT)**
						(exits)	*(exits)*
and of course your father insisted on taking a picture of every damn thing we came across every uh church painting conquistador							
	matador						
what?							
	conquistador's the soldier guy the matador's the guy with the cape ho ho toro! toro!						
alright							
whatever you name it Sam snapped it							
		pardon me for wanting to remember the things I've shared with the woman I love *(takes her hand)*					
			(drinks) it sounds great mom sounds like Barcelona was really great				
(smiles) yeah yeah …it was pretty fucking rad							

WOMAN #1	MAN #1	WOMAN #2	MAN #2	WOMAN #3	MAN #3	GIRL	BOY
(kisses SAM on the cheek)	*(laughs)*	*(laughs)*	*(laughs)*				
						JACKIE	**SAMMY**
						(enters)	*(enters)*
		hey guys we're in public	well here they are			PEW PEW PUCKOOO BAM BOOM EXPLOOOSION!	BOOM BOOM BANG BOOM BANG BOOM POOOWWWW!
			Jackie cut it out				
						(they do kiddish karate moves)	
							BEWARE THE SAMMY-RAI
						AND NIIINJACKIE!	
						YAH YAH YAH	YAH YAH YAH
you know it was quieter when they were fighting			Maddie you think you can prevent your son from further corrupting my daughter?				
		uh yeah Rob sure Jackie's an innocent Sammy's a– hey no uh los ninos no way					you ready for chair battle?
						BRING IT	
							CHAAAAIR BATTLE
		(gives a look)				*(she scurries around)*	*(he scurries around)*
			well I'm gonna get another drink does anyone else want another drink?				
			what? it's a holiday this is what people do on a				

WOMAN #1	MAN #1	WOMAN #2	MAN #2	WOMAN #3	MAN #3	GIRL	BOY
			holiday				
		uh wow okay					
			you know what I've already got a wife, Mad				
		do you Rob? cuz no one's seen her for a while					
			oh so now I'm supposed to take relationship advice from you?				
						(they start to chair battle) YAHHHH	YAHHHH
		guys hey both of you cut it out go back outside and play huh?					
							but we're out of firecrackers! *(bangs the table)*
	hey	too bad				yeah we blew em all up! BANG! *(bangs table)*	BOOM! POW!
			Jackie				
who the hell gave them fire crackers?		you're going					
	it's the fourth! that's what kids do on the fourth!						what about my corn dog?
						yeah what about our corn dogs?	
		we'll come find you when dinner's here okay?				dad?	
			listen to your aunt				
		bye! byeeeeee!					
						BEEEEOOOO–	SHAPOOOOM– *(he runs off)*

WOMAN #1	MAN #1	WOMAN #2	MAN #2	WOMAN #3	MAN #3	GIRL *(she runs after him)*	BOY
(SHIFT)	(SHIFT)	(SHIFT)	(SHIFT)	(SHIFT)	(SHIFT)	(SHIFT)	(SHIFT)
		god it's just they grow up so fast		**JACKIE** *(enters)*	**SAMMY** *(enters)*		
you're telling me					mom hey mom		
			speak of the devil *(drinks)*	hi daddy sorry we're late *(kisses his cheek)*			
			it's okay honey have a seat		mom mom hey mom		
		what is it Sammy I'm talking you're interrupting me why are you always interupting me?					
					I'm just letting you know I'm gonna be out past curfew later you told me to tell you if I was gonna be out past curfew so here I am telling you …jeez		
		fine					
					you're such a spaz		
	hoo big plans tonight, *(a little racist)* Sammy-rai?						
					(a little racist) hooooo with your blessings Grandpa Sam-sei		
	(laughs)		*(weird look)*		*(laughs)*		
			(he stands. raises his				

WOMAN #1	MAN #1	WOMAN #2	MAN #2	WOMAN #3	MAN #3	GIRL	BOY
			glass. he may chime it a little too aggressively. drunk.)				
			hey! hello! …in honor of Turkey Day in the spirit of giving thanks I would like to share what I am thankful for				
					(snickers) booze		
					what?		
				(rolls her eyes)			
			(holding it together) …okay well uh my family I am so very thankful for my incredible family				
					(snickers)		
			excuse me?				
					you're excused		
			do you have something to say?				
					(gives a look)		
go ahead, Robbie							

WOMAN #1	MAN #1	WOMAN #2	MAN #2	WOMAN #3	MAN #3	GIRL	BOY
			uh *(tries to laugh it off)* now where was I?				
					Orlando		
			what?				
		Sammy					
					uh		
					aren't you always in Orlando instead of with your incredible family? *(laughs)*		
			(ROBBIE *nearly explodes)*				
			okay listen to me you ungrateful little shit your mother might not be interested in disciplining you but that doesn't mean you get to do or say whatever you want you have to learn some respect you have to learn a little decorum				
		hey			hey		
		Robbie			whoa		
		this is my son					
	hey hold on						
			this is your family and you need to show them the love and patience they show you no no you keep my wife out of this				
					like anyone knows what that means		
					oh hey speaking of family where's Aunt Steph? yeah hey Jackie where's your mom? what does she not like hanging out with us anymore? are we not all perky enough for her or something?		
		look guys it's Thanksgiving					
					I'm just asking a question		

WOMAN #1	MAN #1	WOMAN #2	MAN #2	WOMAN #3	MAN #3	GIRL	BOY
				grow up Sammy	grow some tits Jackie		
			(he grabs Sammy by the arm. quiet.) how dare you				
he's drunk you're drunk		this is unacceptable absolutely unacceptable			whoa *(laughs)* people are looking I mean you are totally embarrassing yourself		
			(he lets go of **SAMMY**'s *arm)* you know it's no wonder your father left	dad come on he's just being a brat			
		jesus christ Rob			seriously? is that supposed to hurt my feelings?		
			look at what you're doing to your mother				
		hey					
		hey	you think this has been easy on her?				
		leave him alone			yeah leave me alone		
		(to **SAMMY***)* don't you dare say another word			*(zip the lip motion)*		
			god Maddie you have no idea how to handle anything do you?				
		no!		*(there are people watching)*			
maybe Sammy should stay with Darius for a while		no! I don't need you no					

WOMAN #1	MAN #1	WOMAN #2	MAN #2	WOMAN #3	MAN #3	GIRL	BOY
	now I'm not sure that's such a good idea	I can handle this myself!					
			I'm just trying to help				
Maddie honey I mean it it might be for the best		I don't need help					
		I'm not some damsel in distress I am a grown woman! I don't care if you like the way I live my life it's my life okay? IT IS MY LIFE!					
		ow *(she feels under her armpit)*					
			are you okay?				
		(a suspended moment)					
		why's it so hard?					
			it's gonna be okay				
		why's it feel so hard?					
maybe you should see a doctor							
			Maddie look at me hey it's all gonna be okay				
		I'm sorry, Robbie					
			no hey hey just look at				

WOMAN #1	MAN #1	WOMAN #2	MAN #2	WOMAN #3	MAN #3	GIRL	BOY
			me				
		mom					
		dad					
we're right here							
			look at me				
		(she turns to her son)					
		Sammy…					
					mom?		
		oh					
		oh!					
		<u>CLANG</u>					
		(MADDIE *is served a giant plate of hot food on a heavy plate. she eats and eats. she exits when finished.)*					
(SHIFT)	**(SHIFT)**	**(SHIFT)**	**(SHIFT)**	**(SHIFT)**	**(SHIFT)**		
					mom?		
					mom?		
	(shattered)						
	(he takes **NICOLE**'s *hand.)*						
(shattered)							
Maddie…							
			(deeply shaken)				
			…no				
			…god				
			…no				

WOMAN #1	MAN #1	WOMAN #2	MAN #2	WOMAN #3	MAN #3	GIRL	BOY
					no		
					no		
	I…		Maddie				
	I never…						
Sammy here							
come here darling							
				I'm right here, Sammy, seriously if you need anything			
					no		
Sammy					no		
					mom		
honey come here							
Sammy							
please–							
					no no no no		
(she beckons the family to hold hands. they do. **NICOLE** *leads them in prayer.)*							

WOMAN #1	MAN #1	WOMAN #2	MAN #2	WOMAN #3	MAN #3	GIRL	BOY
our Father who art in heaven hallowed be thy name Thy kingdom come Thy will be done on earth as it is in heaven Give us this day our daily bread And forgive us our trespasses, As we forgive those who–	our Father who art in heaven hallowed be thy name Thy kingdom come Thy will be done on earth as it is in heaven Give us this day our daily bread And forgive us our trespasses, As we forgive those who–		our Father who art in heaven hallowed be thy name Thy kingdom come Thy will be done on earth as it is in heaven Give us this day our daily bread And forgive us our trespasses, As we forgive those who–	our Father who art in heaven hallowed be thy name Thy kingdom come Thy will be done on earth as it is in heaven Give us this day our daily bread And forgive us our trespasses, As we forgive those who–	*(he very noticeably does not pray)* you know what? you know what you know what! *(he stands. he berates the rest)* you didn't care about her none of you cared no shut up just shut up! she was my mom, okay? she was my mom and and none of you gave a shit you could have like tried to raise money or like given up your jobs to be with her you could have like stopped your lives is it so hard to like stop your life for just like a second? it's like everyone goes back to their lives so	our Father who art in heaven hallowed be thy name Thy kingdom come Thy will be done on earth as it is in heaven Give us this day our daily bread And forgive us our trespasses, As we forgive those who–	our Father who art in heaven hallowed be thy name Thy kingdom come Thy will be done on earth as it is in heaven Give us this day our daily bread And forgive us our trespasses, As we forgive those who–
			Sammy buddy–				

WOMAN #1	MAN #1	WOMAN #2	MAN #2	WOMAN #3	MAN #3	GIRL	BOY
					quickly they barely take a breath before it's like back to normal		
					we should take the time you know we should take the time to like not be assholes you're all just a bunch assholes!		
					this whole this whole country is just a bunch of fuckin assholes! everyone's just sitting around and talking and not doing a fuckin thing about all the hurt and pain and like bad shit that's going down all over the world and I'm tired of just sitting here and talking I wanna do something about it I wanna go out there and do something about it and if that means I have to like sign up and kill a few people kill a few assholes to do it then fine then I'll go sign up and kill a few assholes so people will understand that it doesn't have to be like this		
					we can be better and I'm gonna show you I'm gonna show all of you assholes she was my mother		

WOMAN #1	MAN #1	WOMAN #2	MAN #2	WOMAN #3	MAN #3	GIRL	BOY
					so stop looking at me		
					like that		
					I'm going okay?		
					I don't care what you		
					say I'm gonna make a		
					difference		
					cuz I'm sick of it I'm		
					so sick of it		
					I just want it to be		
					different that's it I just		
					want it all to be		
					different		
					<u>**CLANG**</u>		
					(he is served a big		
					plate of food. he eats		
					and eats. everyone		
					averts their eyes.		
					there's nothing to		
					say really. he exits.)		
					(long, long,		
					long pause.)		

(SAM *and* **NICOLE** *are left alone…*
…everything begins to move much, much slower now…)

WOMAN #1	MAN #1	WOMAN #2	MAN #2	WOMAN #3	MAN #3	GIRL	BOY
(SHIFT)	**(SHIFT)**						
(she wears a tiny							
yellow ribbon)							
(pause)	*(pause)*						
		what are you thinking					
		of getting?					
I don't know, Sam							
(pause)		*(pause)*					
		these menus keep					

WOMAN #1	MAN #1	WOMAN #2	MAN #2	WOMAN #3	MAN #3	GIRL	BOY
	getting bigger and bigger						
mm							
(pause)	*(pause)*						
Robbie called							
	oh yeah? what'd he say?						
not much he was at one of Steph's conferences							
(pause)	*(pause)*						
	how's Jackie?						
she got some kind of award at her high school							
	for what?						
he didn't tell me							
(pause)	*(pause)*						
	did he mention the pictures?						
what pictures?							
	from their visit						
oh no why would he, Sam?							
	I thought he'd say						

WOMAN #1	MAN #1	WOMAN #2	MAN #2	WOMAN #3	MAN #3	GIRL	BOY
well he didn't							
(pause)	*(pause)*						
	hm?						
what?							
	did you say something?						
(she shakes her head)							
	I think I might get the salmon						
(SHIFT)	**(SHIFT)**						
(pause)	*(pause)*						
Robbie called							
	when?						
this morning							
(pause)	*(pause)*						
	Nicole						
what?							
	why didn't you tell me?						
you were asleep							
	I was not						

WOMAN #1	MAN #1	WOMAN #2	MAN #2	WOMAN #3	MAN #3	GIRL	BOY
I called to you							
(pause)	*(pause)*						
	well what'd he say?						
he's got a new job							
	oh yeah? does he like it?						
he hasn't started yet							
(pause)	*(pause)*						
	how's Jackie?						
she's fine							
	did she get our present?						
I don't know, Sam							
(SHIFT)	**(SHIFT)**						
(the yellow ribbon is now gone)							
(pause)	*(pause)*						
	hey how's your sister?						
my sister?							
	yeah she still in restaurants?						
she's… she's gone Sam you know this							

WOMAN #1	MAN #1	WOMAN #2	MAN #2	WOMAN #3	MAN #3	GIRL	BOY
(pause)	*(pause)*						
	then who's gonna watch the kids?						
(smiles at **SAM**. *takes his hand.)*							
why don't we order?							
(pause)	*(pause)*						
(SHIFT)	**(SHIFT)**		**(SHIFT)**				
			(enters)				
			ROBBIE sorry I'm late				
	whoa ho ho! Robbie!						
			how are you?				
we're good we're just so happy to see you							
			hi mom *(kisses her cheek)* dad uh happy anniversary …what a run huh?				
	how long are you staying?						
			(he adjusts his watch. smiles.) you know how it is can I get you guys something to drink?				

WOMAN #1	MAN #1	WOMAN #2	MAN #2	WOMAN #3	MAN #3	GIRL	BOY
I'm on							
	well we'll make the most of it won't we? where's uh where's Jackie?		*(drinks)*				
			she's uh backpacking with her friends in Norway then Iceland next week				
wow exotic							
	I hear they eat whale there now don't tell me that's a shellfish! *(laughs.)*						
			uh huh				
it's very exciting							
	big change of scenery from Massachusetts						
			Connecticut, dad she goes to school in Connecticut				
	are you sure?						
			yeah I write the checks so				
(pause)	*(pause)*		*(pause)*				
have you heard from Steph?							
			(bristles) mom please *(drinks)*				
(SHIFT)	**(SHIFT)**		**(SHIFT)**	**(SHIFT)**			

WOMAN #1	MAN #1	WOMAN #2	MAN #2	WOMAN #3	MAN #3	GIRL	BOY
				(enters, wearing her compass necklace)			
				JACKIE hey hi			
Jackie! oh darling! look at you all grown up! my god! you're so beautiful! and you're wearing the necklace I gave you! how wonderful!	whoa ho ho!						
				thanks			
				this? oh yeah huh			
	well have a seat						
				oh sorry I can't stay my boyfriend's plane just got in and he lost his luggage so he's *(gestures)*			
	at least have some coffee, Maddie, or–						
			dad				
				this is Jacquelyn			
	of course it is! what'd I say?						
you said Maddie							

WOMAN #1	MAN #1	WOMAN #2	MAN #2	WOMAN #3	MAN #3	GIRL	BOY
	so? what's wrong with that?						
Sam							
				shit I'm already late sorry it's so nice to see you guys			
	now Madeleine						
Sam			dad				
				(she leaves)			
	I'll say what I want leave me alone! lemme be lemme be uh what						
here let me							
	what						
here	what uh don't touch me						
sh	I can don't leave me alone						
*(she tucks a napkin into **SAM**'s shirt)*	I don't want you touching me						
	(The plate arrives. No clang.) *(**NICOLE** feeds **SAM**. she takes her time.)*						
			(he watches this for a long while) so look I know this is bad timing, mom				

WOMAN #1	MAN #1	WOMAN #2	MAN #2	WOMAN #3	MAN #3	GIRL	BOY
			but				
			uh–				
			(he stands. finishes his drink.)				
			hey				
			let me pay for this				
			okay?				
			that helps right?				
			if I pay?				
when are you coming back?							
			I don't know				
			(he adjusts his watch)				
			things are pretty crazy				
			what with the lay off				
			and uh				
			well				
			I met this woman this				
			amazing woman				
			Maddie would've…				
			…Maddie would've				
			loved her				
			she's got a lotta spunk				
			and uh kids				
			and they're great kids				
			a great family				
			so				
that's wonderful							
			it's all a little too much				
			right now				
			but you should really				
			come out and visit				
			sometime				
			it's nice				

WOMAN #1	MAN #1	WOMAN #2	MAN #2	WOMAN #3	MAN #3	GIRL	BOY
I'm sure it is							
			…well…hey…soon okay?				
			I'll be home again soon				
			…I love you				
			(he kisses **NICOLE**. *turns to his father. with regret…)*				
			bye dad				
			(he leaves)				
(long pause. the pace slows down considerably. **NICOLE** *continues to feed* **SAM**.*)*							
…my god where does the time go? *(a little laugh to herself.)* where does it all go? …oh Sam I will never forget the day we… the day we… I will never…ever…							
		*(***SAM*** begins to eat by himself)*					
oh Sam Sam my Sam							
(she watches him eat)							

WOMAN #1	MAN #1	WOMAN #2	MAN #2	WOMAN #3	MAN #3	GIRL	BOY
Sam							
Sam							
Sam							
	(and **SAM** *slowly recedes from view)*						
(long pause)	*(long pause)*						
(SHIFT)		**(SHIFT)** *(enters wearing necklace)* **JACKIE** Grandma?					**(SHIFT)** *(enters)*
is that?							
is that Jackie?							
		hey Grandma					
my god							
look at you							
Jackie							
you look just like your							
mother							
		(smiles) yeah thanks					
it's been so long							
how are you?							
		I'm good					
		I'm					
		well					
		I want you to meet					
		someone					

WOMAN #1	MAN #1	WOMAN #2	MAN #2	WOMAN #3	MAN #3	GIRL	BOY
		this is Matthew Matthew this is your great grandmother Nicole …she gave me this when I was little like you *(gestures to necklace)*					
							MATTHEW hi
		he's a little shy					
he's precious *(she touches the boy's hair)* oh! a great grandchild! my god! to see the day! *(she is upset)* we started something didn't we? we really started something							
			are you okay? Grandma?				
(she stares off)							
			hey why don't we eat, huh?				

WOMAN #1	MAN #1	WOMAN #2	MAN #2	WOMAN #3	MAN #3	GIRL	BOY
		Grandma? oh now where where's that server?					
							she's probably hiding from you, mom
		oh yeah? why's that?					
							cuz she's playing a trick on you?
		and what kind of trick might that be?					
							a funny trick
		funny how?					
							funny like a surprise
		oh yeah?					
							yeah she's maybe hiding on a shelf in the kitchen while you're like "where is she?" "when's she gonna get here?" until you think about it so much that you forget and once you forget she's gonna sneak up on you when you're not thinking about it in her special server sneaking shoes really slowly

[handwritten: YOUR FINE! Cheat out]

WOMAN #1	MAN #1	WOMAN #2	MAN #2	WOMAN #3	MAN #3	GIRL	BOY
							sneak
							sneak
							sneak
		then what?					sneak
							mmm
							then she's gonna take your order
		and what am I gonna order?					
							mmmm
							everything
		everything?					
							yeah
							cuz it's been so long
							and you're so hungry
							that when you finally
							get the chance to order
							you're gonna get
							everything on the
							menu
		that's a lot					
							well it seems like a lot
							but when you really
							think about
							it's not so much
		yeah					
		I guess not					
		I think you might be					
		right					

WOMAN #1	MAN #1	WOMAN #2	MAN #2	WOMAN #3	MAN #3	GIRL	BOY
							I know I'm right
		I love you					
							you don't have to get cheesy, mom
		(cheesy voice) I love you so much					
							(laughs) mom
		now say goodbye					
							bye Grandma Steph
		no honey Steph's my mom like I'm your mom this is my Grandma Nicky like Grandma Steph's your grandma					
							it's a lot to remember
		that's okay …say goodbye					
							goodbye lady
		(laughs) goodbye lady					
							goodbye lady
		(she begins to recede from view) goodbye lady					*(he begins to recede from view)*
							goodbye lady

WOMAN #1	MAN #1	WOMAN #2	MAN #2	WOMAN #3	MAN #3	GIRL	BOY
		goodbye lady					
		(fainter and fainter)					*(fainter and fainter)*
							goodbye lady
		goodbye lady					
							goodbye lady
		goodbye lady					
							goodbye lady
		…goodbye					
		(she's faded away…)					*(he's faded away…)*
(but NICOTE remains. the table is hers and hers alone.							
she waits and waits and waits							
but the wait is so so long…)							

THE END